CULTURE SMART!
IRAN

Stuart Williams

·K·U·P·E·R·A·R·D·

First published in Great Britain 2008
by Kuperard, an imprint of Bravo Ltd
59 Hutton Grove, London N12 8DS
Tel: +44 (0) 20 8446 2440 Fax: +44 (0) 20 8446 2441
www.culturesmartguides.com
Inquiries: sales@kuperard.co.uk

Culture Smart! is a registered trademark of Bravo Ltd

Distributed in the United States and Canada
by Random House Distribution Services
1745 Broadway, New York, NY 10019
Tel: +1 (212) 572-2844 Fax: +1 (212) 572-4961
Inquiries: csorders@randomhouse.com

Copyright © 2008 Kuperard

Series Editor Geoffrey Chesler
Design Bobby Birchall

ISBN 978 1 85733 470 8

British Library Cataloguing in Publication Data
A CIP catalogue entry for this book is available from the
British Library

Printed in Malaysia

Cover image: Ornamental tile work in mosque, Isfahan. © *Javarman/Dreamstime.com*
Images on pages 39, 52, 96, 120, and 134 by courtesy of the author.
Images on pages 123 and 124 (top) by courtesy of Fariborz Kiani of Nava Arts, UK.
Images on pages 14 © Shervin Afshar; 22 © Photo Ginolerhino; 24 © Fabienkhan;
33 © Mostafa Saeednedad; 34 © Moshino31; 40 © Philippe Chavin; 47 © Sepehrnoush;
55 © Pentocelo; 56, 89 (bottom) © Hamed Saber; 78 © Bertil Videt; 89 (top)
© Zoom Zoom; 105 © tannaz; 107 © Danielle E. Sucher; 127 © Juergen Lehle; and
148 © Zereshk.

About the Author

STUART WILLIAMS is a British journalist specializing in financial and current affairs. A graduate in German and Russian from Worcester College, Oxford, he has worked in Frankfurt as bureau chief for AFX News and as a senior editor for Agence France Presse (AFP) for Europe and Africa in Paris, and for the Middle East in Cyprus. He has covered elections and militant attacks in Russia from Moscow, and Israel's war against Hezbollah in summer 2006 from Beirut. Stuart first traveled around Iran as a tourist after leaving university and was immediately entranced by a country that appeared so different from its image abroad. Having attempted to learn a serviceable Persian, he now works for AFP in Tehran.

The Culture Smart! series is continuing to expand.
For further information and latest titles visit
www.culturesmartguides.com

The publishers would like to thank **CultureSmart!**Consulting for its help in researching and developing the concept for this series.

CultureSmart!Consulting creates tailor-made seminars and consultancy programs to meet a wide range of corporate, public-sector, and individual needs. Whether delivering courses on multicultural team building in the USA, preparing Chinese engineers for a posting in Europe, training call-center staff in India, or raising the awareness of police forces to the needs of diverse ethnic communities, it provides essential, practical, and powerful skills worldwide to an increasingly international workforce.

For details, visit www.culturesmartconsulting.com

CultureSmart!Consulting and **CultureSmart!** guides have both contributed to and featured regularly in the weekly travel program "Fast Track" on BBC World TV.

contents

contents

Note: The book uses the conventional English transliterations for Persian names, e.g. Hossein rather than Hussein (but the Arabic form for Saddam Hussein), Mohammad rather than Mohammed, etc.

Map of Iran

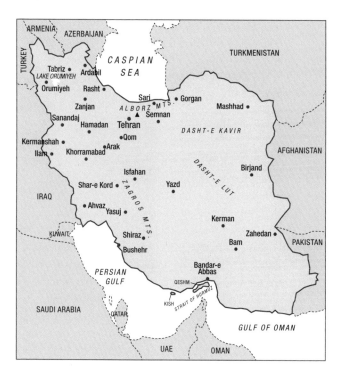

introduction

Iran these days is rarely out of the headlines. Accused by the West of seeking to make a nuclear weapon, its growing power in the Middle East has been the subject of much scrutiny and concern.

The West's fascination with Iran is nothing new. For centuries, foreigners have been entranced by a land that has an exotic, eastern, and even mystical allure and is quite distinct from other countries in the region. Iran's best-known export—the Persian carpet—has always attracted buyers for its whiff of mystique. Travelers have been seduced by the echoes of an extraordinary ancient history contained in the word "Persia."

But beyond the clichés and the stereotypes, what is the real Iran like at the start of the twenty-first century? For sure, the country still offers romance and the exotic. It is a place where people sing medieval poetry on mountaintops. Where the bread is never more delicious than when it is baked early in the morning. Where the intricate patterns of Islamic art thrill visitors of whatever religion.

But Iran is also a modern society that is experiencing great change. The country is still feeling the effects of the Islamic revolution of 1979—a true revolution in the sense that it completely changed the country's political orientation within days. The revolution imposed strict rules on social behavior, and all women must cover themselves, alcohol is prohibited, and the mixing of unrelated couples is banned. Iran is now the archenemy of the United States, not its ally. But the image of a reactionary, strict society only goes part of the way. Social restrictions have loosened considerably in the last years. Today strict Islamic rules coexist with an increasingly dynamic society being driven by an overwhelmingly young population. Animosity toward the West at a political level sits side-by-side with a wholehearted welcome for foreigners as individuals.

This book aims to show how life in Iran really is and how visitors can feel comfortable in its society. It explains the basic culture of a country full of surprises. Despite Iran's deep commitment to Islam, the pre-Islamic Zoroastrian past is still part of everyday life. Its language, Farsi, shares the same linguistic roots as English or French. It is a country where one of the more genuine democracies in the Middle East is overlaid by an unelected theocracy. And where "no thank you" really does sometimes mean "yes please."

The only way to break through the stereotypes is to visit the country and experience modern Iranian culture firsthand. *Iran keshvar-e jadouyi-e* (Iran is a magical country) is how many Iranians sum up this entrancing, beautiful, and sometimes infuriating place. If nothing else, it is a country whose inhabitants genuinely wish visitors *Khosh amadi*!—Welcome!

Key Facts

Official Name	The Islamic Republic of Iran (*Jomhouri-ye Eslami-ye Iran*)	Iran became an Islamic Republic after the 1979 Islamic revolution that toppled the US-backed shah.
Capital City	Tehran	Pop. around 7 million; incl. suburbs and satellite cities 12 million
Main Cities	Iran's second city is the holy city of Mashhad (pop. 3 million)	Other big cities include Tabriz, Isfahan, and Shiraz.
Population	70.47 million (2006 census). Population growth is 1.61%.	68.5% live in urban areas, compared with around 22% in 1940.
Area	636,296 sq. miles (1,648,000 sq. km)	The highest point is Mount Damavand, at 18,606 ft (5,671 m).
Climate	Hugely varied. The Caspian Sea region has up to 78.74 inches (2,000 mm) of rain a year, while the interior desert areas are dry almost all year. The north has freezing winters; temp. on the Persian Gulf can reach a sticky 104°F (40°C) in summer.	The wettest main city is Rasht, the driest is Yazd. The hottest is the coastal city of Bandar Abbas, and the coldest is the northern city of Ardebil.
Language	The main language is Persian (Farsi), written using the Arabic alphabet with slight modifications.	Minority languages include Azeri, Kurdish, Arabic, and Armenian.

Religion	The state religion is Islam. The overwhelming majority of Iranians adhere to the Shiite branch. A minority of Iranians are Sunnis.	Other recognized minority religions are Christianity, Judaism, and Zoroastrianism. The Bahai faith is not recognized.
Government	Since the Islamic revolution a mix of theocracy and democracy. The top political figure is the supreme leader, a cleric. Under him are a president and a parliament.	Elections held every four years for the president and the parliament. The supreme leader is chosen and supervised by a clerical body elected by the people.
Dress Code	Women must wear the Islamic headscarf and cover all bodily contours in public.	Men should not wear shorts, except when playing organized sports.
Currency	The rial (IRR): 1 rial=100 dinars. 10,000 rials are worth around US $1.	Transactions are often carried out in tomans (1 toman=100 rials).
Media	Television is state-run. Several channels available in most cities. Satellite TV is banned but widely watched in Tehran and other urban centers.	Iran has a lively Persian-language press scene but newspapers are still subject to strict controls and liberal publications have frequently been banned.
Electricity	200 volts, 50 Hz	2-pronged plugs used
Telephone	Iran's country code is 98.	To dial abroad out of Iran, dial 00.
Time Zone	GMT + 3.5 hours in winter, GMT + 4.5 hours in summer	Daylight saving time was restored in summer 2008.

LAND &
PEOPLE

GEOGRAPHY AND CLIMATE

Straddling the frontiers of Europe and those of South and Central Asia, it is hardly surprising that Iran encompasses a huge diversity of cultures and landscapes. It has western borders with Turkey, possibly a future European Union member. To the northwest lie the former Soviet republics of Armenia and Azerbaijan. There is a northern border with the reclusive former Soviet republic of Turkmenistan and then the Caspian Sea, a major economic asset. When the Soviet Union collapsed in the 1990s, Iran found the number of its northern neighbors had tripled.

To the west, its neighbor is one-time foe and now close ally Iraq. Further south are the sultry waters of the Persian Gulf, across which lies the Arabian Peninsula. To the east, Iran borders desert regions of Pakistan and further north Afghanistan, a wild area that is notorious for banditry and drug trafficking.

As a result of this extraordinary geographic position, it is sometimes hard to define Iranian culture. On occasion it appears very eastern and even mystical, while at others historic links to

Europe and the West are more evident than elsewhere in the region. Regional influences and minority groups have also left substantial traces.

Climate
Iran's weather is one of the country's greatest assets and it is sorely missed by the millions who now live in the diaspora. Iranians will proudly tell you how it is possible on the same day to be sweltering by the Persian Gulf while a friend is battling below freezing temperatures climbing a mountain in the north. The weather varies greatly from region to region throughout the year. *Iran chahar fasl-e*! (Iran has four seasons!) is a proud and often-repeated refrain. And it is true, the country has spectacular weather: normally sunny, with short but intense periods of rain or snow.

The capital Tehran has the full kaleidoscope of weather—heavy snowfalls in the winter (starting in December) usually cause chaos in the city center but delight skiing fans who flock to several resorts within a short drive north of the city.

Spring breaks around March with occasional but heavy showers. True summer starts in May, with temperatures kept bearable in Tehran and several other cities by their high altitude. Fall is a long and beautiful season in the capital with stable, sunny weather often lasting into November. In the winter months temperatures can plunge to -4°F (-20°C) in the north of Iran, and even in central Tehran prolonged periods below freezing are common. By contrast, the temperature in Tehran can rise over 86°F (30°C) in summer; on the humid littoral cities of the Persian Gulf temperatures in excess of 104°F (40°C) are common in summer.

Landscape
The landscape of Iran is of breathtaking diversity. The northern provinces bordering the Caspian Sea are relatively lush areas with high precipitation that burst into bloom in springtime. The contrast with the two deserts that make up around one-third of the country could not be

greater. The massive Dasht-e Kavir that starts east of Tehran and the Dasht-e Lut that heads toward the Pakistan border are areas with sand dunes and endless scrubland that may seem more familiar in Arab and African countries. As well as these deserts, there are also great mountain ranges. The Alborz Mountains that rise high above Tehran include Iran's highest peak, Mount Damavand, an extinct volcano rising to 18,606 feet (5,671 m), whose huge cone is one of the country's iconic images. Extending down the country's western edge like a massive spine is the long Zagros range, the other main chain of mountains.

Iran has a huge interior lake in its north, Lake Orumiyeh. On the Persian Gulf, Kish and Qeshm islands are being heavily promoted by the authorities as tourist destinations.

POPULATION

Iran's majority population is Persian (*Fars*), who still proudly see themselves as the descendants of the great Achaemenian empire that ruled Iran and much of the region between 550 and 330 BCE. They speak Persian (Farsi), a language of Indo-European origin (see more in Chapter 9). Persians adhere to the Shiite branch of Islam.

According to the latest census, the population is around 71 million. There has been drastic population growth and a move from villages to towns over the last half century, utterly changing the social makeup and population density.

Ethnic and Religious Minorities

Iran is also home to several ethnic minorities, reflecting its position between a number of cultures. The largest minority are ethnic Azeris (*Azari*, though often referred to by all Iranians as Turks), a Turkic people who have substantial populations especially in the north and northwestern provinces as well as Tehran. The Azeri population in Iran is substantially larger than that in the neighboring state of Azerbaijan itself. Speaking a Turkic language, the Azeris also adhere to Shiite Islam and are generally very well integrated into society. Supreme leader Ayatollah Ali Khamenei is himself the son of Azeri parents.

There are also substantial Kurdish populations in the western provinces, with their own distinctive culture and clothing (baggy trousers for men and colorful head scarves for women). They are generally Sunni Muslims. Concentrated in the western Khuzestan province is an Arab population consisting of a mixture of Sunnis and Shiites. The Sunni Baluch form a large population in the Sistan-Baluchestan province that borders Pakistan and Afghanistan. Other important ethnic minorities include the Turkmen. There is also a substantial nomad population in Iran, although the numbers living a truly nomadic life have dropped sharply since campaigns to settle them in the 1920s and 1930s.

Few people outside Iran are aware that religious minorities exist within its strict Islamic system. The Islamic Republic's constitution recognizes and guarantees the right to freedom of worship for Christians, Jews, and Zoroastrians. All these groups have their own members of parliament and their own cultural centers. It is, however, strictly forbidden for Muslims to convert to other religions.

The largest Christian community is the Armenians (*Aramaneh*), a group who have lived in the territory of Iran for centuries. Despite numbering only around fifty thousand, they are prominent in professional trades and their churches are easy to spot in major centers like Tehran, Isfahan, and Tabriz. Visitors will also see shop signs in the unique Armenian script in their quarters. There are also smaller populations of Assyrian and Chaldean Christians.

Iran's Jewish (*Yahudi*, or *Kalimi* for specifically Iranian Jews) population is the largest in the Middle East outside Israel. However, the current number of around twenty thousand is well below the approximately one hundred thousand from before the revolution. Although President Ahmadinejad and other officials have launched virulent tirades against Israel, the authorities insist that their only objection is to Zionism, and that Iranian Jews have full rights and freedoms. Jews in Iran are often prominent and successful in the bazaar trade. The Islamic Republic has always refused to recognize Israel, which was a close ally of the pro-US imperial Iranian regime.

Zoroastrians (*Zartoshti*) adhere to the religion that was dominant in Iran before the Arab invasion in the seventh century. Contrary to popular belief, Zoroastrians are not fire worshipers, although fire appears in their rituals and temples symbolizing life, growth, and purity. There are tens of thousands of Zoroastrians in Iran, although again numbers have been hit by emigration.

Iran's biggest minority before the Islamic revolution were the Bahais, who advocate the unity of all religions. However, the Islamic authorities deem Bahais to be apostates and the group is not recognized by the constitution as a religious minority. Bahais have none of the rights enjoyed by other minorities and those remaining are forced to pursue their faith underground.

A BRIEF HISTORY

Iranians are proud of their history and no foreigner will feel at ease in the country without some understanding of its past. Many Iranians still see themselves as the direct descendants of the Persians who built one of the greatest empires in world history 2,500 years ago.

The name "Iran," which is now applied to the modern, ethnically diverse country, has ancient roots, coming from the word "Aryan," in reference to the Indo-Europeans who entered the country in around 1000 BCE. Iran was for long called "Persia" (*Fars*) in the West, although strictly speaking this is a rendering of the name of the southern Iranian province of Fars (which is still known as such) from where the Achaemenian Iranian kings ruled.

The country also witnessed just three decades ago one of the most important events of modern times, the Islamic revolution of 1979 that ousted the pro-US shah, Mohammad Reza Pahlavi, and ended 2,500 years of monarchy in Iran.

Early Times

Pottery dating from 5000 BCE is evidence of a lively early culture in Iran. There are also indications of urban societies forming as early as around 3000 BCE, such as Tepe Yahya, an archaeological site in the eastern Kerman province. By 2000 BCE civilization appears to have been flourishing in Iran, as shown by the impressively elaborate bronze and copper work found at Tepe Yahya and Shahdad in the same region.

A growing civilization was meanwhile developing in southwest Iran, around the modern Khuzestan province on the border with Iraq, in the region known as Elam. It was in Elam that one of the first great cities of Iran, Susa (*Shoush* in Persian), was built, a capital that would later be expanded by the great Achaemenian kings. The sophistication of their culture is shown by the clay tablets in a proto-Elamite script that have been found in the area as well as accomplished metalwork. It was in the Elamite period that the great ziggurat temple of Choqa Zanbil was built, the remains of which still stand today—it is the best-preserved such site in the region. Elamite civilization appears to have reached a high point around 1500–1100 BCE but was badly hit by the

invasion of the famous Babylonian king
Nebuchadnezzar at the end of the twelfth century
BCE. But archaeologists have found increasingly
sophisticated and innovative examples of bronze
work and pottery from the years 1100 to 500 BCE.

Many of the great treasures of this and other
periods of ancient Iranian history
are to be found in
Europe, rather than
Iran. For example, a
large number of the
objects excavated at
Susa are now in the
Louvre in Paris. Looting
and colonial rule in the

nineteenth and early twentieth centuries mean
that many treasures from Elamite, Achaemenian,
and Sasanian Iran are held in the Louvre and the
British Museum in London—something that still
rankles modern Iranians. Nevertheless the
National Museum in downtown Tehran still boasts
an impressive collection.

The Persian Empire
The Achaemenian kings who ruled from 550 to
330 BCE are the most famous rulers of ancient
Iran. They built a great empire that at its height
stretched from Libya to India and remains a
source of great pride for Iranians today.

By 600 BCE a people known as the Medes had
won control of an area around their main city of
Ecbatana, the site of the modern city of Hamedan.

They even helped the Babylonians overthrow the Assyrians and sacked their great cities of Nineveh and Nimrud. But in 550 BCE the Median king was deposed by Cyrus the Great, the most famous of all Iranian kings, and the Achaemenian dynasty began. In a fantastic and rapid series of conquests, Cyrus seized large swathes of Lycia and Anatolia in modern-day Turkey in the 540s BCE. In 539 BCE Cyrus captured the great city of Babylon, allowing him to take over much of that empire, including Palestine and Syria.

Cyrus is still revered by many Iranians today. He was the author of the "Cyrus Cylinder," a clay cylinder inscribed with Babylonian cuneiform, where Cyrus describes himself as "king of all the world" and relates how Babylonians were free to worship their gods after their conquest. Some have called the cylinder (held in the British Museum) the world's first declaration of human rights. Cyrus was killed in 530 BCE while on a campaign. His monumental tomb at his capital of Pasargadae (near the modern city of Shiraz) is still standing.

After his death, Cyrus's successor Cambyses succeeded in conquering Egypt. Darius I then took the empire's frontiers to India and it was under his rule that the empire reached its greatest extent. He even built a canal between the Red Sea and the Nile. But his most famous legacy is his building at the city of Persepolis (known in Persian as Takht-e Jamshid) near modern Shiraz. Many of the doorways, stairways, and reliefs of Achaemenian

soldiers and other figures still stand and the site is one of Iran's greatest tourist attractions.

But it was also under Darius that the Graeco-Persian wars started and with them the decline and fall of the Persian empire. Seeking to make inroads into Greece, the Persians found their match at the hands of the Greek states, which successfully halted the great expedition of Xerxes I, Darius's successor, in 479 BCE. Weakened both militarily and culturally, the Achaemenians could not withstand the invasion of Alexander the Great in 334 BCE.

The achievements of the Achaemenian empire still arouse strong passions. Some Iranian men still proudly bear the first names of Darioush (Darius) or Sirous or Koroush (Cyrus). The 2006 US film *300* about the Graeco-Persian wars that caricatured the

ancient Persians as little more than bloodthirsty sadists sparked great anger in Iran—both from the government and among ordinary people.

Alexander the Great

Alexander overthrew the last Achaemenian king Darius III in 330 BCE. He is still reviled in Iran for his decision to destroy the buildings at the capital of Persepolis after his invasion. After his death in 323 BCE, Alexander was followed in ruling Iran by his general Seleucus who founded the Seleucid dynasty, under which Greek influence grew.

Parthians, Sasanians, and the Conversion to Islam

A nomadic Iranian tribe overthrew the Seleucids in the third century BCE and its kings became known as the Parthian dynasty. The Parthian kings, most notably Mithradates II, continued to grab territory, extending their hold as far as the Euphrates River. The Parthians were overthrown in 224 CE by the Sasanian dynasty, who were to rule Iran for the next four hundred years.

Until then, the ancient Iranian religion of Zoroastrianism had been widespread in Iran but the Sasanians were the first Iranian dynasty to proclaim it the state religion. Most people in Iran converted to Islam after the Islamic conquest but, as we have seen, there is still a Zoroastrian minority to this day.

The Sasanian king Shapur I (240–72) was known for his religious tolerance and allowed Jewish, Christian, Manichaean, and Mandean minorities to worship freely. However, this was not the case under his successors. Under Shapur I, the Sasanian empire reached its greatest extent, with frontiers on the Euphrates River to the west and the Indus to the east.

Although less famous than the Achaemenians, the Sasanians were equally adept at conquering and also left behind an impressive legacy of ancient sites such as their former palaces at Firouzabad in southern Iran and Ctesiphon in Mesopotamia. There are also stunning relief carvings such as those at Taq-e Bustan in

Kermanshah province as well as works in silk, silver, bronze, and glass. Such was the demand, that Sasanian cut-glass objects were even traded as far as Japan.

But from 637 the Sasanian empire suddenly and rapidly collapsed after being defeated by the invading Arab armies. They brought with them a new religion—Islam—which was to change the course of Iranian history forever.

The Spread of Islam and Shiism

Islam spread rapidly in Iran, perhaps indicating the weakness of the Sasanian dynasty on the eve of the Arab conquest. Islam had split into the Shiite and Sunni sects over a dispute as to who should succeed its founder, the Prophet Mohammad, who died in 632. Muslims who became known as Sunnis favored the caliphs, politically appointed nobles, to succeed

Mohammad. Shiites, however, saw the succession to Mohammad as coming through his bloodline, starting with his cousin and son-in-law, Ali. When Ali's second son Hossein claimed the leadership after his death, he and his followers were massacred at the Iraqi city of Karbala on the order of the caliph Yazid in 680. Shiites still mourn this event fervently in streets and houses across the Middle East on the tenth day (*Ashura*) of the first Muslim month (*Moharrem*). (See Chapter 3.)

So-called "Twelver" Shiites, like those in Iran, recognize twelve imams stemming from Ali. The last of these—the twelfth imam, also known as the Mahdi—is believed to have disappeared into a state of "occultation" in 939. Shiites believe that he will return to the world to usher in a new era of harmony and justice—a belief that is key to the politics of President Mahmoud Ahmadinejad.

Today, Shiites form the overwhelming majority in Iran and are also the majority in neighboring Iraq. There are further Shiite populations in Bahrain, Kuwait, Lebanon, Egypt, Pakistan, and Saudi Arabia. But Iran, which was ruled by a succession of tribal dynasties after the conversion to Islam, did not become a Shiite state immediately. Shiites existed in Iran but Sunni worship was also widespread. It was only in 1501 that a new dynasty—the Safavids—ousted the Mongols who were then ruling Iran and began to zealously establish Shiism as the state religion.

The emerging Shiite state in Safavid Iran rapidly became a counter and a rival to the neighboring Sunni Ottoman empire. The two sides fought numerous battles, further cementing the establishment of a Shiite identity in Iran.

As well as the monumental switch in religion, Safavid Iran also saw the building of road links, the

expansion of industry, and an increase in diplomatic and trade links with the outside world. Its most famous ruler was Shah Abbas (1587–1629), during whose reign the great religious buildings and palaces in the imperial capital of Isfahan were completed. Finally sapped by the continuing wars against the Ottomans, Safavid Iran was conquered by the Afghans in 1722.

While Islam was rapidly absorbed, Iran was the only country in the first wave of the Arab conquests to retain its own language. Iranians are proud of their preservation of Persian, whose grammar bears little relation to Semitic Arabic. Shiism, a minority Muslim sect, has also given Iran a religious identity distinct from its Arab neighbors.

The Qajars

In 1796 another tribal dynasty, the Qajars, came to power. Their rule, which was to last for the next 130 years, has earned a bad press from historians. Some Qajar monarchs have been seen as cruel, lazy womanizers, akin to the most excessive Ottoman rulers. The first Qajar ruler, Agha Mohammad Khan, is said to have plucked out the eyes of twenty thousand men from the city of Kerman. During the Qajar era, the great powers Britain and Russia began a long struggle for control over the country they had realized was of crucial strategic importance.

The noted Russian playwright Aleksandr Griboyedov was killed in Tehran by a mob in 1829 while on a diplomatic mission after seizing women from the imperial harem. The most prominent shah from the Qajar years, Naser ad Din, ruled ineffectually for forty-eight years. Concessions were also handed to Britain to exploit Iranian resources, starting a dangerous trend.

But if the shahs had other interests, reform did take place during this period at the hands of sometimes highly able bureaucrats. Naser ad Din's long-serving prime minister Amir Kabir founded the first schools of higher education and imposed economic reforms—even today his achievements are recognized in the name of Tehran's most prestigious technical university. Amir Kabir, who the shah had murdered while taking a bath, is one of the few administrators from the pre-Islamic Republic era whose name is still honored today.

Meanwhile, the state was forced to cancel a concession given to the British for Iranian tobacco in 1891 after mass demonstrations, the first time in Iran's history that protests had forced a government to back down. The tyrannical Qajar rule eventually led to pressure from dissatisfied merchants and clerics that resulted in the drawing up of Iran's first constitution and the convening of its first parliament in 1906. The movement known as the Constitutional Revolution ushered in the modern era.

Iran's Last Shahs, the Pahlavis

Dissatisfied with the weak rule of the Qajars, Britain in 1921 orchestrated a military coup, led by an officer of humble origins who had risen to command the Cossack brigade, Reza Khan.

Thus started one of the most controversial political careers in Iranian history. Forcing the creation of a new government, Reza Khan became war minister in 1921, then prime minister in 1923. In 1925 he declared himself shah and renamed himself Reza Pahlavi, after an ancient Persian language. Parliament voted for the abolition of the Qajar monarchy with only four against.

Drawing inspiration from Turkey's secular leader, Ataturk, Reza Shah embarked on a campaign to modernize Iran economically, socially, and militarily. He reformed the army, introduced a new legal system, and worked to spread education. But his authoritarian rule left very little room for political debate. One of his most controversial moves was in 1936 to force women who wore the Islamic veil to go bareheaded. His police forces ripped off the head scarves and *chadors* (all-enveloping cloaks) of women who defied the order, something that the state media frequently remind Iranians of today.

Britain, meanwhile, was growing frustrated with Reza Shah's increasingly pro-German and even Nazi sympathies. Infuriated by his continued toleration of German agents in Tehran, Britain forced him to abdicate in favor of his son, Mohammad Reza Pahlavi, in 1941.

Mohammad Reza shared his father's authoritarian streak but few of his strengths. His rule saw massive spending to make Iran a great military power, the promotion of ties with the West, and a program of land reform. His so-called "White Revolution" sought to modernize Iran through land reforms, the spread of literacy, and improvements in women's rights. However, the reforms failed to create an affluent agricultural class and encouraged mass migration to the cities.

A monumental challenge to his rule came in 1953, when the Iranian prime minister, Mohammad Mossadeq, nationalized the oil industry to the fury of Iran's British and US patrons. Mohammad Reza fled the country, but Mossadeq was overthrown in a

CIA- and British-backed coup that allowed him to return.

Mossadeq's defiance made him a hero for many Iranians. His secular tendencies meant his name was rarely mentioned in the early years of the Islamic Republic, but the current standoff over Iran's nuclear program means he is once again being recognized.

In 1971 the shah staged an outrageously lavish celebration at the Achaemenian capital of Persepolis to mark what was touted as the 2,500th anniversary of the monarchy in Iran and where he sought to

portray himself as the natural successor of Iran's ancient rulers. The event symbolized Mohammad Reza's excesses and his ignorance of the growing problems of the urban poor.

Though he had labeled himself *shahanshahi* (king of kings), a mere eight years later he would be overthrown.

The Islamic Revolution and War with Iraq

The shah became increasingly unpopular as the growing numbers of urban poor saw no solution to their problems. Dissent was crushed with increasing brutality by the secret police (SAVAK). The shah was overthrown in 1979 by a coalition of socialists, liberals, and Islamists led by the charismatic cleric Ayatollah Ruhollah Khomeini.

Khomeini had been a fierce critic of the shah since the 1960s and had been imprisoned, exiled to Iraq, and then France. He returned to Iran to declare his vision of an Islamic state. With the shah overthrown,
Khomeini moved to sideline opponents of this vision and Iran became the Islamic Republic of Iran. Khomeini was the supreme leader of the revolution, a position that, according to the new constitution drawn up

after the revolution, would always be held by a learned cleric. This idea of clerical leadership in state politics, or *velayat-e faqih* (guardianship of the jurist; pages 52–3), was one of the key ideas behind the formation of the Islamic Republic.

In complete contrast to the time of Reza Shah, veiling for women became compulsory and Islamic *sharia* law was imposed. But the new constitution also envisaged a presidency and a parliament that were to be directly elected by the people, albeit subject to certain controls. Thus the modern Iranian state is a combination of theocracy and democracy. While the West criticizes Iran for lacking freedom, its leaders still insist the country is a religious democracy (*mardomsalari-ye dini*).

The first years of the revolution were tumultuous. The Islamic Republic's new leaders were targeted in bombings and assassination attempts by opponents of the regime who were still in hiding in Iran. All opposition was ruthlessly suppressed, and there were many executions. In late 1979 a group of Islamist students seized the US embassy in central Tehran and held its staff hostage for the next 444 days. The seizure reinforced the power of the Islamist radicals and also created a breach in relations with Washington that has yet to be mended.

In 1980 the Iraqi dictator Saddam Hussein invaded Iran's southwestern Khuzestan province, which has an Arab population, in the hope of gaining possession of the oil-rich region. This resulted in a bloody eight-year war that is estimated to have cost a million lives on both sides. A successful Iranian tactic for repelling Iraqi advances was to send waves of often young volunteers on potentially suicidal missions into enemy fire. Iran finally accepted a UN resolution calling for a ceasefire in 1988, with both sides accepting a border agreement that had stood since 1975. War affected everyone in Iran due to food and fuel shortages and missile attacks that also hit

Tehran. Few today do not know someone killed or wounded in the conflict. Saddam Hussein was notorious for his use of poison gas against Iranian troops, which has created a legacy of health problems for thousands of veterans. His hanging in 2006 was greeted with jubilation in Iran.

Reconstruction and Reform

When Khomeini died in 1989, his president, Ali Khamenei, was chosen to succeed him as supreme leader. Iran embarked on a period of reconstruction (*sazandegi*) under its pragmatic new president, Akbar Hashemi Rafsanjani, who sought economic recovery after the destruction of the war. Some of the stricter social measures were softened but the economic recovery was marred by inflation and unemployment. Ties with the United States remained nonexistent and those with Europe thorny. Relations with Britain were cut for several years after Khomeini in 1989 issued a *fatwa* (edict) imposing a death sentence on the writer Salman Rushdie for his book *The Satanic Verses*.

After Rafsanjani had served the maximum two four-year terms as president, Iranians astonished the world in 1997 by choosing the reformist cleric Mohammad Khatami as his successor. For many of his young and often female

supporters, Khatami offered the chance of a new start in a country with a booming youth population and he won a landslide victory. But while the smiling and articulate cleric impressed many in the West with his talk of a dialogue of civilizations, his attempts at broader political and social reform within Iran's Islamic system (*nezam-e Eslami*) were stymied by powerful hardliners. In any case, Iranian reform (*eslah*) was primarily aimed at economic change and promoting foreign investment, accompanied by cautious social reforms. Despite winning a new mandate in 2001, Khatami left office in 2005, openly admitting he had failed to fulfill the hopes invested in him.

Ahmadinejad

Another election shock came in 2005 when Iranians elected conservative Tehran mayor Mahmoud Ahmadinejad (until then completely unknown outside Iran) as Khatami's successor. He crushed Rafsanjani in a runoff vote, winning the election on a mandate of promising to help Iran's poor finally feel the benefits of the wealth of OPEC's number two oil producer. Early in his

presidency, Ahmadinejad caused a storm by saying that Israel was doomed to disappear and downplaying the

Holocaust. His style of diplomacy also raised eyebrows, as when he fired off personal letters to US President George W. Bush and German Chancellor Angela Merkel. But most importantly, Iran headed into a standoff with the West over its nuclear program by reversing the suspension of sensitive activities agreed under Khatami.

The nuclear drive was a shah-era project that had been mothballed in the early years of the revolution and then revived after Khamenei became supreme leader. Whereas the West accused Iran of developing technology that could be used to make a nuclear weapon, Tehran insisted it was only seeking to provide electricity for its growing population. Ahmadinejad vowed, often in highly colorful language, never to back down on the issue and the UN Security Council imposed its first-ever sanctions against Tehran. The United States also refused to rule out military action.

Meanwhile, inflation increased and economists blamed Ahmadinejad for injecting excessive cash into the economy to fund local infrastructure projects. But the president, who proclaimed his government to be one of social justice (*edalat*), insisted he was doing all he could for the poor.

The Revolutionary Guards
The Revolutionary Guards of the Islamic Revolution (*Sepah-e Pasdaran-e Enghelab-e Eslami*) were formed shortly after the revolution to merge several paramilitary forces and counter the power of the regular army. They are known to

most in Iran simply as the *Pasdaran* (Guards). They are the most significant and most skilled military force in Iran and are regarded as its ideological army. Iran's best military hardware, including the Shahab-3 long-range missile that can reach Israel and southern Europe, is under their auspices. The Revolutionary Guards also control the *Basij* (Gathering), a volunteer militia claimed to number 12 million people. The head of the Guards is chosen by the supreme leader. With their own land, sea, and air forces, they played a key role in the eight years of the Iran–Iraq war and have remained prominent in all military areas ever since. It was they who sparked a crisis with Britain in 2007 with the capture of fifteen British sailors accused of trespassing into Iranian waters.

In recent years the Guards have expanded their activities in all areas of Iranian life. President Ahmadinejad, himself a former member, promoted several former officers to cabinet posts. Dozens of MPs are former Guards, as is the mayor of Tehran. As well as political influence, they have considerable economic clout, and their economic subsidiaries have seized major contracts in the energy, transport, and engineering sectors.

CITIES
Tehran
For most foreigners, Tehran is their first taste of Iran and it is not always the most palatable. A seething, polluted, traffic-filled metropolis, it is not

an easy experience. The city has grown at a frenetic pace over recent years, putting a great strain on the infrastructure. The traffic, even by the standards of the Middle East, is abominable and during busy times it is possible to be stuck for ages in motionless jams. The architecture is largely modern and uninspiring, with the exception of a

few historic buildings in the south and north of the city. But Tehran has its redeeming features. It is the center of cultural life, and on a clear day the view to

the north of the Alborz Mountains rearing up immediately above the city is spectacular. Tehranis also make up for the cold severity of the urban architecture with real warmth and hospitality. There are also a dozen or so very well-tended parks in the city center to escape from the chaos outside.

Isfahan

Isfahan is the ancient imperial capital of Iran built by Shah Abbas. It has the great Islamic and Persian architecture that Tehran painfully lacks and is a favored destination for foreign tourists. The massive Naqsh-e Jahan Square, one of the largest in the world, is surrounded by a spectacular array of architecture. There are also impressive bridges and

an atmospheric Armenian quarter. Nevertheless,
liberal Tehranis are prone to look down on
Isfahanis as conservative.

Qom

Qom is the clerical epicenter of Iran, home to the
shrine of Massoumeh, the sister of the eighth
Shiite imam, Imam Reza, and where the late
Ayatollah Khomeini lived. Religion is all-pervasive
here, and the city is dominated by clerics and
seminary students and only very few women do
not wear the all-enveloping black *chador*.

Mashhad

The holiest city of Iran, Mashhad, is home to the
shrine of Imam Reza and is an important Shiite
pilgrimage center. The city is also by far the
largest urban conurbation in eastern Iran and its
people are seen as canny operators, with many in
positions of power throughout the country.
Tehran's current mayor, Mohammad Baqer
Qalibaf, hails from Mashhad.

Shiraz

The great city of southern Iran, Shiraz is a favorite with foreign visitors for its laid-back atmosphere and proximity to the great sites of Achaemenian Iran, such as the city of Persepolis and the tomb of Cyrus the Great at Pasargadae. It is also beloved of Iranians for its associations with the great medieval Persian poets Hafez and Saadi, who still exert a huge influence on Persian culture and are both buried in Shiraz.

Tabriz

The main city of the Iranian north, and freezing in winter, Tabriz has close trade and travel links to neighboring Turkey, and the Turkic Azeri language is more common here than Persian. While the city has few great monuments save an outstanding bazaar, it is situated in one of Iran's most beautiful regions.

Yazd

On the fringes of the desert in central Iran, Yazd is renowned for its still-inhabited and perfectly preserved mud-brick medieval city. Its maze of warrens and beautiful mosques are one of the great attractions of Iran. It is also the hometown of the former president Mohammad Khatami and is famous for its delicious sweets.

chapter two

VALUES & ATTITUDES

THE IRANIAN PSYCHE

National pride plays a huge role in what it means to be Iranian. Occupying a key position in the

Middle East, Iranians will always be swift to remind foreigners that they are not Arabs. The country is surrounded by Arab and Turkic states, giving Iranians a feeling of being unique in their own region. The atmosphere in the country is strikingly different from that of the Arab states, however near they may be. Iranians are very conscious of their own ancient history—there is a continuous connection between land and people going back thousands of years. Iranians will constantly refer back to the glories of the Persian empire as they still feel strongly this was achieved by their direct ancestors.

Iran is still a traditional society and religion plays a vital role in the identity of most of its people. The call of the mosque or a banner proclaiming love for an important religious figure is never far away. The fact that most Iranians adhere to the Shiite branch of Islam makes them feel distinct from the Arabs, most of whom belong to the majority Sunni denomination.

But Iranian society—unsurprisingly for a country of more than 70 million people and home to a number of different ethnic groups—is hugely complex. Indeed, making generalizations about this country is a risky business that has ensnared many foreigners who believe they have understood the national psyche. Despite the international perception of Iran as a religiously conservative society, there is far more to the country than this.

Iranians have a range of passionately held beliefs, interests, and pastimes. First-time visitors to Iran are almost always struck immediately by how lively urban society is; the streets are a gallery of exuberant activity. Music of all kinds, Western and traditional, blares out. People chatter away in a never-ending banter, the young try to impress with their style. Visitors should find people of both sexes who are ready to discuss (almost) any subject. Prepare to have any preconceptions about an unexciting, reactionary society well and truly dispelled.

RELIGION
Religion in Daily Life
The overwhelming majority of Iranians, normally estimated at more than 80 percent of the country's population, belong to the Shiite branch of Islam. As said above, for many people, whatever their

political persuasion, being a Shiite Muslim is a fundamental part of being Iranian. Just because someone is Westernized, liberal, and secular does not mean that their religion is not an important part of their identity. Conversely, it would be wrong to assume that someone who is ostentatiously devout, possibly a turbaned cleric or a *chador*-clad woman, is inimically hostile to the West.

On religious holidays, shopkeepers rush out into the streets to offer free drinks, fruit, and cake,

while the mosques are full all day long. If you visit a major mosque on such a day, you will have a striking indication of the importance of religious belief to Iranians. It goes without saying that you should dress conservatively and behave modestly but generally even on these intense occasions Iranians are happy to welcome foreigners who show respect.

Atheists should bear in mind that Iran is not a good place to express their beliefs. Firstly, it is illegal to do so in the Islamic Republic. More importantly, Iranians in general, from all sections of society, believe in God (*Allah* in Arabic, but Iranians often use the Persian word *Khoda*) and would be both astonished and perhaps even terrified by any suggestion that God does not exist.

Shiites and Sunnis

That Shiism is so important to the national psyche is perhaps explained by the fact that Shiites form a minority within Islam, estimated to be between 10 and 15 percent of the world's Muslim population. Shiites in Iran and elsewhere have customs, festivals, and rites that would be unrecognizable to adherents of Sunnism, the majority branch of world Islam.

As we have seen, the schism between the two sects dates from a disagreement over the successor to the founder of Islam, the Prophet Mohammad, after his death in the seventh century. Shiites recognize the Prophet's cousin and son-in-law, Ali, as his successor and thereafter the direct descendants of Ali. Sunnis, however, believed that political leadership and respect within the community were the most important prerequisites for a successor and recognized the rulers known as caliphs who went on to form the Umayyad dynasty in Damascus.

The first Sunnis were happy to separate religious and political authority, whereas Shiites believed that only the most exceptionally holy people could lead the Islamic community after the death of the Prophet. One and a half millennia later, the latter concept remains crucial to understanding how politics works in modern Iran.

For Shiites, the direct descendants of Ali, known as the imams, provide the necessary guidance for people to live in accordance with the precepts of God. The twelve imams are a feature of Shiite Islam that has no parallel in Sunnism. Iran sees scenes of fervent devotion during the holidays that mark the birthdays or death anniversaries of the main imams. (See Chapter 3.)

The Mahdi, Lord of the Age

Another special feature of Shiite Islam is the emphasis on the twelfth and final imam, known in Iran as the Mahdi or *imam-e zaman* (lord of the age). According to Shiites, the Mahdi is in a state of occultation after being hidden by God from the physical world in the tenth century. Shiites fervently believe in and wish for the Hidden Imam's return, which they believe will herald the end of time and the beginning of a new age of divine justice. In Iran, any mention of the name of the Mahdi is usually followed by the words *Ajalallah ta'ala farajah*, "May God hasten his return."

The importance of the Mahdi has increased even more in Iran following the 2005 election of the deeply religious Mahmoud Ahmadinejad as president. Ahmadinejad is a fervent believer in the imminent return of the Mahdi. He has repeatedly said in political speeches that his presidency is paving the way for the return of the Hidden Imam and he accuses the West of having no faith that the era of justice is about to dawn. Such an emphasis has not been universally popular with Iran's elite. Previous administrations put far less political emphasis on the apocalyptic predictions associated with the Mahdi's return. One top

Iranian cleric, Hassan Rowhani, complained that this approach led to an increase in superstition to the extent that people were putting out food in case the Mahdi should return that very night.

The Cult of Martyrdom

Any visitor to Tehran cannot fail to notice the huge murals painted on the sides of office blocks and apartment buildings, frequently in prominent positions by major roads. Often brilliantly executed, they show fresh-faced young men with inscriptions in Persian. These men are the "martyrs" (*shahid*) of the eight-year war against Iraq, which came at a crucial stage early in the Islamic revolution and remains key to the national psyche today.

Hundreds of thousands of men died in the war and their sacrifice is repeatedly hailed in speeches and ceremonies by Iran's leaders today. In Western countries such a loss would be seen principally as tragic, but in Islamic Iran such "martyrdom" (*shahadat*) is seen as glorious and beautiful. A heroic death takes the soul to a blissful afterlife. This difference in cultural perceptions of conflict may demand a degree of sensitivity from the foreign visitor. In Iran, martyrs are to be worshipped, as shown by the cemetery for the fallen of the Iraq war (Behesht-e

Zahra) just outside Tehran where a fountain eternally spouts red water symbolizing blood.

The war is known in Iran as the war of "Sacred Defense" (*Defa-ye Moghaddas*) and it is an incontestable historical fact that it was started when Saddam Hussein's forces invaded Iran's oil-rich west—Iranians will be very angry if you suggest otherwise. Many people you meet will have taken part in the war or lost loved ones.

The idea of martyrdom is encountered in other aspects of life and death in Iran. State media describe victims of a deadly traffic accident on the dangerous roads as martyrs. The same goes for members of the security forces who are killed in gunfights with drug smugglers or militant groups in Iran's border provinces. Also known as martyrs are the several top Iranian leaders who were killed in a wave of bomb attacks by the outlawed armed opposition group the People's Mujahedeen in the immediate aftermath of the Islamic revolution.

The concept of the *shahid* goes back to the early days of Islam and the emergence of the bloody schism between Sunni and Shiite Islam. The most renowned martyr of all is Imam Hossein, who was killed at the battle of Karbala in Iraq and whose death is still marked each year by the impassioned *Ashura* ceremony.

Shrines
Also special to Shiite Islam are shrines, which are the burial places of the imams and other important religious figures. Neighboring Iraq, which has a

majority Shiite community, has a number of important shrines, most notably in the cities of Najaf, Karbala, Baghdad, and Samarra. Iran also has

sites of great significance, the most holy being the shrine of the Shiite Imam Reza in Mashhad, which draws millions of pilgrims annually from all over the

world. Reza (known in Arabic as Ali al-Rida) is the eighth imam of Shiite Islam and the only one to be buried inside the borders of today's Iran.

Another major site is the shrine of Massoumeh, Imam Reza's sister, in the central city of Qom.

Khomeini has his own shrine just outside Tehran, a huge complex visible from the road to the new international airport. Impressive from the outside, it is unfinished and a little underwhelming within.

NATIONAL PRIDE

Along with the intensity of religious belief, national pride is the other unmistakable characteristic of Iranians, as we have seen. All states in the Middle East show impassioned national pride, but in Iran it is something special. Pride in the country's ancient civilization, its natural beauty, and its cultural achievements is the one thing that unites all Iranians, whatever their political views and irrespective of whether they live inside the Islamic Republic or in the diaspora.

This national pride is shown in the questions that almost every Iranian will put to visitors about their experiences in the country and whether they

were positive. They will be sure to ask whether you have seen its most famous ancient sites, like the ruined Achaemenian capital of Persepolis or the former imperial capital of Isfahan. They will also want to know how Iran compares with foreign countries.

Days when the national soccer team is playing also show the intensity of this passion. Major victories—few and far between in recent years— like the win against Bahrain in 2005 that qualified Iran for the World Cup are marked by barely contained rejoicing.

A reason perhaps for the intensity of national pride is the sense of historical continuity that modern-day Persians feel between themselves and their ancient past. Iranians see what their leaders always refer to as the "great nation of Iran" (*mellat-e bozorg-e Iran*) as going back thousands of years to the great Persian empire founded by Cyrus the Great in the sixth century BCE.

ABERROU

Nothing is more important in both the private and public life of an Iranian than pride. The notion is taken much more seriously than in the

West and an episode that causes the loss of pride or "face," even if there is no material loss, is regarded as a catastrophe. In Iran, the idea is strongly conveyed by the word *aberrou*, which literally means "water of the face." Losing your *aberrou* in front of others is seen as an unmitigated disaster and Iranians of all classes will go to sometimes extraordinary lengths to ensure this does not happen. This can become very frustrating for outsiders, who may be given elaborate excuses rather than the truth just so that an Iranian can hold on to their *aberrou*. But in Iran, this is seen as perfectly normal and not lying in any way.

FATE

Fate (*sarnevesht*) is another concept that may seem very abstract to outsiders but takes on a very real meaning in Iran. Even Iranians who do not profess to be religious can talk passionately about fate. The idea that the story of your life is somehow preordained (or "written ahead," which is what *sarnevesht* means) is hugely potent throughout Iran. Iranians will often see signs of fate in events that have allowed them to escape injury or death by what seems to be chance.

ATTITUDES TO FOREIGNERS

Iranians generally adore foreigners. The country has had a long history of contacts with the West and it is only in recent years that it has found itself increasingly isolated on the international scene. Foreigners have a degree of novelty value in Tehran that they do not have on the streets of Cairo or Dubai. People stop, look, want to ask questions. This may seem aggravating but the curiosity is relaxed and not in the least aggressive. Most foreign visitors leave Iran with a positive impression of the friendliness and hospitality of its inhabitants. They may even find themselves mobbed (in the nicest possible way) at famous tourist sites, with school groups excitedly asking questions and even begging for autographs.

Media coverage of Iran can sometimes give the impression of a society hostile to foreigners, but a quick stroll round any Iranian city—even somewhere very conservative such as clerical Qom—rapidly dispels these stereotypes amid smiles and handshakes. Of course, there are still sensitivities, and showing respect for the religious and national values outlined above will ensure that no offense is caused.

While almost all Iranians enthusiastically and genuinely welcome any foreigner (including Americans), many are also extremely bitter about the role played by Western governments in their country's history. They may even directly blame the West for ruining their business or failing to respect Iran's history.

For many, the country's potential has been held back by foreign states, either because of the invasions throughout its history or, in the previous century, the great powers' cynical rush to exploit its oil wealth. One date particularly etched in the mind of Iranians is the 1953 CIA- and British-inspired coup that toppled Prime Minister Mohammad Mossadeq after he nationalized Iran's oil industry to wrest it from foreign control.

The same applies to the current international standoff over Iran's nuclear program, which the United States accuses of being a cover for an atomic weapons drive. Many Iranians of all political stripes will vigorously defend the country's right to atomic energy and are genuinely perplexed by what they see as another Western attempt to deprive Iran of technology and thwart its development.

But most Iranians, whatever their views, are happy to draw a line between politicians and ordinary people, meaning foreign visitors can feel at ease. Many upper-middle-class Tehranis have relations living in the United States and Europe and can prove to be surprisingly familiar with these societies.

So Westerners are normally assured of a warm welcome. However, Iranians show far less respect toward the hundreds of thousands of Afghan refugees and migrants living in the country. Millions of Afghans have taken refuge in Iran over the past decade to escape the conflicts in their home country. They work on building sites and carry out menial jobs that no Iranian would be seen doing. They are often paid the most miserly of wages.

THE IDEAS OF THE ISLAMIC REVOLUTION

Iran's current system of government dates from the
1979 Islamic revolution (see Chapter 1). After the
ousting of the shah, Khomeini moved quickly to
suppress his erstwhile secular and liberal allies who
did not share his worldview. Iran became an
Islamic Republic (*Jomhouri Eslami*) whose laws
and politics were based on Islam.

Two decades after his death in 1989, Khomeini's
personality and political vision still dominate Iran.

His piercing eyes
stare out from every
banknote, his
portrait hangs in
every shop, his
speeches are
broadcast almost
daily on state
television. The
country follows
sharia law and strict Islamic values of clothing and
behavior must be observed by the people in every
area of public life.

Criticism of "Imam Khomeini," as he is referred
to, is strictly prohibited. Massively charismatic,
Khomeini was a complex figure who remains
poorly understood in the West. Possessed of an
extraordinary will to impose his vision, he was not
without pragmatism when required.

Khomeini's political legacy is the system that
runs the Islamic Republic, a highly personal vision
known as the *velayat-e faqih* (literally, guardianship

of the jurist). According to this system, the state is led both politically and religiously by a highly qualified cleric, who acts as guardian for the community in the absence of the twelfth imam. In line with this vision, Khomeini appointed himself supreme leader of the Islamic revolution (*rahbar-e moazzem-e enghelab-e Eslami*). On Khomeini's death, he was succeeded in this position by the then president Ali Khamenei. Beneath the supreme leader, there are a number of bodies who work in line with the *velayat-e faqih*—the all-clerical Assembly of Experts (*Majles-e Khobregan*), which selects the supreme leader and is elected once every eight years, and the unelected Council of Guardians (*Shura-ye Negaban*), half of whose members are chosen by the supreme leader.

ISLAMIC VALUES, MODERN ATTITUDES

Iran has some of the strictest Islamic laws in the Middle East (with the exception of Saudi Arabia) but, ironically, perhaps the most colorful and diverse society in the region. Visitors often find that the picture of Iran they encounter as tourists or business travelers bears no resemblance to the "Axis of Evil" state portrayed in the Western press.

There *are* restrictions for sure. Women must cover their heads and all bodily contours. The consumption and sale of alcohol are strictly prohibited anywhere. Dancing is frowned upon and mixed-sex parties with Western music are illegal and sometimes the target of police raids.

Sexual relations outside of marriage are forbidden and theoretically punishable by jail sentences or even death. As in other Middle Eastern countries, kissing or other such contacts between partners in public is a complete no-no. Homosexuality is also strictly illegal (see more on page 102). Satellite television is banned as it is deemed to import decadence from abroad. The police regularly seize the dishes that are nonetheless a regular feature on some Tehran rooftops.

Iran executes more criminals annually than anywhere in the world other than China. Executions in Iran are almost always carried out by hanging. In recent years they frequently took place in public, until a 2008 decree by the head of the judiciary effectively put a stop to this. Amputations and even stonings to death are allowed by law, if rarely carried out in practice.

However, this is not the whole story. Iran has loosened up considerably since the late 1990s thanks to reforms, albeit cautious, and the effects of its huge youth population. The country presents a far more welcoming face to foreigners than in the decade after the revolution, when the streets of Tehran were rocked by terrorism and the country was locked in a war of attrition with Saddam Hussein's Iraq.

The parks are now filled with young couples holding hands and quietly flirting. While many women still opt to wear the all-enveloping black *chador*, others, especially in Tehran, are pushing the limits of what is permissible, wearing figure-hugging coats and head scarves that show ample amounts of hair. Mixed-sex parties, while illegal, do take place. Political discussion can be lively, and it is not unusual for the government to be flayed in the reformist press for its policies.

WOMEN

Don't come to Iran expecting women to be shy, retiring types who never appear in the street. Anyone holding such beliefs will find them undermined pretty quickly. Indeed, within hours of arriving in Iran you are likely to have witnessed a scene like a female car driver giving a piece of her mind to a male fellow driver who she believes cut her off. Many people come to Iran expecting the position of women to be similar to Saudi Arabia, where it is even illegal for

them to drive, but this simply is not the case. Women in Iran are well educated and opinionated, and many have successful careers.

The most conspicuous aspect of women's lives in Iran is the Islamic dress code, under which a woman must cover her head and all bodily contours from the age of puberty onward. There are no exceptions and foreign women must obey the laws like any Iranian. This means female visitors must wear a head scarf and body coat anywhere in public, including hotel restaurants. As in other Islamic countries, the wearing of a *hijab* (head scarf) is seen by the authorities as a way of preserving a woman's dignity and preventing men having sexual thoughts about her in public. In winter, wearing *hijab* should not be too much of a hassle but some feel burdened by the extra clothing in the heat of Iran's summer. However, there is a huge diversity in what women wear on the streets (see more in Chapter 4) and since the 1990s there has been a considerable relaxation over what is permissible.

Iranian men still expect women to do the cooking and clean the house, although richer

families may hire help. A man usually will not help out in the kitchen, beyond doing the garden barbeque—although it's not impossible. The role of the woman in the home remains the traditional one of cook and housekeeper. However, such attitudes have not stopped women leading successful professional careers—they are particularly prominent in medicine, engineering, the law, and science. Women easily outnumber men at the university level, which augurs well for their future influence in Iran.

Prominent Iranian Women

The awarding of the Nobel Peace Prize in 2003 to women's rights activist and lawyer Shirin Ebadi was a major indication of what women can achieve. Ebadi in the 1970s became Iran's first female judge, before women were banned from holding such posts after the revolution. But she was able to resume work as a lawyer and her taking on of sensitive human rights cases has irked the authorities. The

official response to her prize was at best lukewarm.

Another prominent woman from a completely different background and field is Anousheh Ansari: Iranian-born, she made a fortune in telecoms in the United States and in 2006 became the world's first female space tourist. Despite living full-time in the US and holding American nationality, Ansari was an example for many Iranian women of what female ambition could achieve. Hard-liners were less impressed—one conservative daily wondered why there was so much fuss about the "rich woman in space."

Women are starting to make inroads into politics—there are several female MPs and many more on municipal councils. However, the major breakthrough is yet to come. Women occupied only two places in both the Ahmadinejad and Khatami cabinets: the vice-presidents for women's rights and environmental protection. There is also a dispute over whether a woman is constitutionally allowed to run for president, and the post of supreme leader is of course reserved for a man. One of the most prominent female Iranian politicians is Massoumeh Ebtekar: known as "Sister Mary" when she was the spokeswoman for radical students in the 1979–81 US embassy siege, she went on to become a reformist and serve in the Khatami cabinet.

Women's Issues

Women's rights are a vexed issue in Iran. For a woman, blood money (*diyeh*)—the amount relatives can claim if a person is injured or killed in a crime or an accident—is set at half that for a man. A woman's testimony in court is worth half that of a man. Activists in Iran have launched a petition to change these laws known as the "One Million Signatures Campaign." However, its backers face an uphill struggle and have on occasion been arrested by the police. Public women's rights protests are extremely rare in Iran and participants are sometimes arrested for taking part in what is deemed to be an illegal gathering. The occasional and sparsely attended demonstrations held on International Women's Day (March 8) are highly sensitive events and heavily policed.

Moral Crackdown

Stung by the perceived slipping standards, hard-liners in the spring of 2007 launched a moral crackdown, with police targeting women whose dress was deemed inappropriate and other improper behavior. Tens of thousands of women were warned that they were not obeying the dress code, while some men were apprehended for sporting "Western" haircuts or "decadent" clothing. Coffee shops—the traditional meeting places of boys and girls—were shut down and shops selling inappropriate clothing were raided. The police insisted the crackdown was popular with the public at large (something not everyone would agree with) and would continue. "Moral police" vans, marked in Persian as *Gasht-e Ershad* (Guidance Patrol), have become a regular feature in Tehran's major squares. Male and female officers apprehend offenders and if necessary take them to a detention center to be given a written warning. Their parents then bring suitable clothing and they are released. Penalties for repeat offenders are stricter.

But the crackdown does not appear to have affected the dynamism of Iranian street society, which is here to stay. There is still a huge diversity of female dress on display in the streets and coffee shops are packed with couples on Thursday nights ahead of the weekends. There is no comparison with the stricter days of the early 1980s.

chapter three

CUSTOMS & TRADITIONS

Iran's diverse calendar of annual customs and traditions reflects its ancient Zoroastrian past, its Islamic heritage, and the modern revolutionary era. It is a complex mixture of the old and the new. Holidays are extremely frequent in Iran: on average, there will be at least one day a month marking an important religious festival or an event in the country's past.

THE CALENDAR

Iran's calendar is unique and very different from systems used elsewhere in the world. It is one of the most significant relics of the country's pre-Islamic past and still plays an important role in daily life. Don't expect January, February, March to mean much in Iran; you will have to learn the Iranian months and years as it is by these that all business is done.

The Iranian year, which is based on the sun, differs from both the Western solar calendar and the lunar calendar used in the rest of the Muslim world. In both the Persian solar and the Muslim lunar calendars, the years are counted from the flight of the Prophet Mohammad to escape the persecution of Muslims in Mecca to the sanctuary of Medina in 622, known in Arabic as the *hijra*. However, the start of the Iranian New Year is celebrated by a festival that is pre-Islamic in origin (Nowruz: see pages 64–6), marking the start of the vernal equinox, which comes around March 20. Thus the Iranian year between March 2008 and March 2009 is 1387, the year between March 2009 and March 2010 is 1388, and so on. All government and commercial business is done in line with this system, although of course Iranians are aware that the years are counted differently from other systems.

As the Iranian year is based on a solar calendar, important Muslim festivals, most notably the fasting month of Ramazan (Ramadan: see pages 69–71), change dates from year to year. The Muslim lunar calendar had been used extensively in Iran up to the twentieth century. However, Reza Shah made the ancient Persian solar calendar the country's sole calendar. Perhaps surprisingly, this usage has not been affected by the Islamic revolution.

Iranians are proud of their calendar, which is based on astronomical observations and has its own mechanisms for ensuring it does not fall out of synch. They are also proud of its claims to be the most accurate in the world and its origins in

Persian history. The basic structure of the calendar is said to have been designed by a committee led by the great Iranian astronomer and poet Omar Khayyam in 1079. But it goes back further than that: the names of the twelve months in the solar Persian calendar have their origins in the ancient religion of Zoroastrianism. Their existence is perhaps the most obvious example of the continuing influence of Zoroastrianism—now a minority faith in Iran—on the daily lives of people in the Islamic Republic.

Six of the months are named after the metaphysical beings whom the Lord of Wisdom (Ahura Mazda) called upon to defeat hostile spirits. The names of four other months recall the mythological beliefs of the forces in nature that are beneficial to humans (for example, fire and water). One month recalls the guardian angels (*forouhar*) who descended to earth to protect mankind. Another month is named in honor of the Creator, Ahura Mazda, himself.

The names of the months are as follows,
starting with *Farvadin*, the first month of the
Iranian New Year. Iranian months end on around
the twentieth day of a Western month.

Persian Month	Western Months	Named After
Farvardin	March–April	The descent of the guardian angels to earth
Ordibehesht	April–May	Lord of the Fire
Khordad	May–June	Protector of Waters, Health
Tir	June–July	Lord of the Scribe
Mordad	July–Aug.	Protector of Plant Life, Immortality
Shahrevar	Aug.–Sept.	Lord of the Sky, Stones
Mehr	Sept.–Oct.	Force of loyalty
Aban	Oct.–Nov.	Force of waters
Azar	Nov.–Dec.	Force of the fire
Deh	Dec.–Jan.	The Creator, in honor of Ahura Mazda
Bahman	Jan.–Feb.	Protector of Animals
Esfand	Feb.–March	Protector of Mother Earth

If you are spending any length of time in Iran, a
knowledge of the calendar will be essential in
coping with daily life. Sell-by dates on perishable
goods, like yogurts and cheeses, all use the Persian
calendar, while monthly remittances will be
expected by the end of the Persian and not the
Western month. In Iran, the date is printed as

year/month/day, usually using the Arabic numerals
although Latin numerals are now increasingly used
instead. Remember that whereas you read the
letters in Persian from right to left, numerals are
read from left to right, as in English. Bizarrely,
percentages and other digits are sometimes written
from right to left, causing great confusion.

Another good reason for learning the dates is the
Iranians' habit of referring to important events in
their history just by the date and not by what
actually happened. For example, if you hear
someone talking about the *bist-o do-e Bahman* (the
22nd of Bahman), they are talking about the day
when the Islamic revolution ousted Shah
Mohammad Reza Pahlavi. In the same way, if
someone mentions the *do-e Khordad* (the 2nd of
Khordad), it is the day when Mohammad Khatami
stunned the world by winning the 1997 presidential
elections, stoking hopes of change and reform.

ANCIENT PERSIAN HOLIDAYS
Nowruz (around March 20)
Nowruz, literally "New Day," is the Persian New
Year and the most important holiday of the year
for the majority of Iranians. Officially, the first
four days of the New Year are a national holiday
but in practice most people take off a fortnight
and the country shuts down. The richest Iranians
may head abroad but most people stream toward
popular resorts inside the country and make a
succession of family visits, which are obligatory

over the New Year period. Thousands of Tehranis rush toward the north and the Caspian Sea to enjoy the bracing weather, leaving the capital unusually quiet, unpolluted, and for once free of traffic. Doing business is a bad idea at *Nowruz* as most people will be on holiday. It is also quite the worst time for tourists to visit the country as hotels will have been booked up months in advance by Iranians traveling or visiting relations. Transportation tickets will also be hard to come by in this period, with seats on long-distance trains particularly notorious for selling out the instant that they go on sale.

Nowruz is the only pre-Islamic festival still officially commemorated with a holiday in Iran. Some extremist clerics have called for it to be banned but such ideas have never been taken seriously by any government, which celebrates the holiday as enthusiastically as anyone else.

Nowruz marks the exact astronomical beginning of spring and is infused with symbols of renewal as well as Zoroastrian traditions dating back thousands of years. The most important tradition at Nowruz is the *haft seen* (seven "s"s), which correspond to the seven creations of the Zoroastrian faith and the immortals that protected them. Today, all these objects begin with the letter "s" but that was not always the case. They are *sib* (apple), *sekke* (coin), *senjed* (berry), *seer* (garlic), *sabze* (grasses), *serke* (vinegar), and

samanou (a wheat meal). These objects are laid out on a table, where a plant is grown to celebrate renewal. A goldfish may also be bought to celebrate life. A Koran is added and also perhaps a book of poetry by the great medieval poet Hafez or the *Shahnameh* (Book of Kings), Iran's national epic by the poet Ferdowsi. There is also much cleaning of houses to mark the time of renewal. Traditionally, this is the time when all Iranians go out and buy a new set of clothes. This, as well as the general gift-buying, means the traffic in Tehran in the run-up to the festival is even more appalling than usual.

Chaharshanbe Souri (mid-March)
The New Year is preceded by a frenetic evening known as Chaharshanbe Souri (literally, Red Wednesday). This takes place on the last Tuesday–Wednesday night before the New Year and could be described as an Iranian fireworks night. Its origins are not entirely clear, although

the importance of fire during the celebrations has a parallel in Zoroastrianism. Fires are lit all over Iran, with the avowed aim of chasing away bad spirits. For most people, it is an excuse to throw firecrackers, light fireworks, and jump over bonfires. Predictably, people have been known to become over-excited and every year there are reports of injuries from burns or explosions.

In the early days of the Islamic revolution, Chaharshanbe Souri was frowned upon. But the authorities have recently allowed the celebrations to proceed in designated areas, albeit with stern warnings about public safety hazards.

Sizdah be Dah (around April 1)

The New Year period officially ends thirteen days into the first month of Farvardin, with another uniquely Iranian festival celebrating nature, known as Sizdah be Dah (literally, the Thirteenth Outside) and also as the Ruz-e Tabia'at (Day of Nature). This is the day when all Iranians rush outside to go on spectacularly large picnics in nature, which can mean anything from the high mountains to a patch of grass by the roads. Town parks all over the country are filled with families sitting on rugs and drinking tea and eating Iranian specialties—it is one of the most atmospheric days of the whole Iranian year.

ISLAMIC HOLIDAYS
Ashura

The Shiite mourning festival of Ashura (named after the Arabic word for "ten") is perhaps the most important religious day marked in Iran. Coming on the tenth day of the Muslim month of Moharrem, Ashura marks the death of the third Shiite imam, Hossein, at the battle of Karbala in 680 in modern-day Iraq. Seen by his Shiite supporters as the true leader of the Muslims (being the grandson of the Prophet Mohammad), Hossein led a rebellion against the caliph Yazid I. Intercepted at Karbala, Hossein and almost all his supporters were slaughtered by Yazid's vastly more numerous army.

The martyrdom of Hossein still arouses genuine passion and even tears in Iran. These feelings reach their height during the mourning ceremonies of Ashura. Processions go through the streets led by drums and banners. Ashura is the time when the closeness between the Shiite faithful and their imams, even though one-and-a-half millennia have elapsed since the events took place, is particularly apparent.

The pain of the battle of Karbala and Hossein's mortal wounds are still felt as though they happened yesterday. Passion plays (*tazieh*) are staged to re-create the events of the battle, arousing great emotion among the spectators. Shopkeepers will put black mourning banners outside their shops, while taxi drivers have black pennants fluttering from the front of their cars. Many men wear black shirts, a sign of mourning in Iran. Some people flagellate themselves in an effort to empathize with the pain of Hossein and his followers. On occasion, passions during Ashura have run so high that people have been known to scar their heads and draw blood with knives. However, it is wrong to exaggerate this particular custom, which is frowned upon by the authorities nowadays and only practiced by a minority. For most people, Ashura is a time for reflection, prayer, and the family. It is not a celebration, however, and foreigners would be wrong to "congratulate" Iranian friends on the holiday.

Ramazan
Ramazan (Ramadan) is the Muslim holy fasting month. Like all other Muslims, Iranian Muslims are required to refrain from eating, drinking, and sexual activity from dawn until dusk. Seen by

many outsiders as a period of sacrifice, Ramazan is also enjoyed by many Iranians for the time spent with the family and the huge feasts (*eftar*)

that follow the breaking of the fast at sundown. Unlike in many other Muslim countries, in Iran the consumption of food or liquid in public is strictly forbidden by law for everyone during daylight hours in Ramazan. Anyone seen flagrantly breaching this rule will likely have to explain himself to the police.

This makes Ramazan a difficult, though not impossible, time to travel in Iran. While restaurants will refuse to serve Muslims, some eateries in upscale hotels will discreetly serve non-Muslim foreign visitors. Shops are also open all day long throughout the month as normal, so it is easy to stock up on supplies to eat at home during the day. Travelers are exempt from the fasting rules and roadside restaurants remain open to all throughout the day. By no means do all Iranians strictly observe the fast all through the month, though a majority probably do so around the country. The key to enjoying the fast is said to be awakening before dawn for a large breakfast (*suhor*) and then avoiding too much strenuous activity before the evening *eftar* meal. As in other Muslim countries, business is slower in Ramazan and driving more erratic.

The fasting month ends with the Eid ul-Fitr (festival of the Breaking of the Fast), which is usually marked in Iran with a two-day public holiday. There are major religious sermons on these days. But Eid ul-Fitr is also a time for gift giving and eating. This is the time to congratulate Iranians on the festival, known in both Persian and Arabic as an *eid*, by saying "*Eid-e shoma mubarak!*" (Congratulations on the festival!).

Birthday of the Mahdi
This is when Shiites remember their twelfth imam, the Mahdi, who they believe disappeared into temporary occultation in 939 and will return to save the world and usher in a new era of justice. Thousands of people make a pilgrimage to the Jamkaran Mosque, outside the city of Qom, where he was once said to have appeared; from here, they send written messages to the Mahdi.

Arbaeen of Imam Hossein
From the Arabic word for forty, Arbaeen marks the fortieth day (as is traditional in Muslim mourning) after Ashura.

Eid-e Ghorban (Festival of Sacrifice)
This marks the near-sacrifice by Abraham of his son, as recounted the Koran. Those who can afford it sacrifice a sheep at home and distribute the meat among the poor. There are also organizations that take care of the whole process.

The deaths and births of the most important figures in Islam and Shiite Islam such as the Prophet Mohammad, Imam Ali, and the eighth imam, Reza, are also national holidays. The death of a religious figure is known as *rahelat*, the martyrdom as *shahadat*, and the birthday as *veladat*.

ISLAMIC REVOLUTIONARY HOLIDAYS

The third kind of national holiday in Iran relates to the events of the 1979 Islamic revolution.

Day of the Victory of the Islamic Revolution (February 11)

This is the major revolutionary holiday, held to celebrate the day in 1979 when the shah's army refused to intervene to put down the popular uprising against the imperial regime. Although the shah had left Iran three weeks earlier, this is now considered to be the day when he was toppled. The holiday is marked by gigantic rallies of hundreds of thousands of people across the country and much chanting of the mantras of "Death to Israel!" (*Marg bar Israel!*) and "Death to America!" (*Marg bar Amrika!*). Superficially it all sounds very hostile, although nowadays the marches have more of the atmosphere of a fiesta with sports exhibitions, face painting, and balloon displays encouraging families to take part. The ten days leading up to February 11 are known as the *Dah-e Fajr* (Ten Days of Dawn). This period also sees Iran's main film festival, known as the Fajr Film Festival.

Day of the Islamic Republic (March 31)
This national holiday marks the overwhelming support given by Iranians to the idea of declaring Iran an Islamic Republic in a referendum on March 31, 1979.

Death of Ayatollah Khomeini (June 3)
This major mourning holiday marks the death of Khomeini in 1989. Black banners fly above the streets, the papers publish special supplements devoted to the man known simply in Iran as "the imam," and state television relays his speeches. Major ceremonies amid a huge crush of people are held at his shrine south of Tehran, including a speech by the supreme leader.

Week of Sacred Defense (end September)
The week of "Sacred Defense" (Defa-ye Moghaddas) recalls the start of the Iran–Iraq war in 1980, when Iraqi dictator Saddam Hussein invaded western Iran in the hope of annexing the oil-rich and Arab-populated Khuzestan province. His action sparked one of the bloodiest wars in modern history. For Iranians, the war was one of defending the integrity of their historic territory against the Iraqi onslaught.

The week of ceremonies kicks off with a huge military parade in Tehran where most of the country's weapons are on display, including its longer-range missile the Shahab-3 (which can reach the fringes of Europe). The week is a time of rousing speeches from politicians and the military recalling Iranians' readiness to defend their land, something that has gained added pertinence amid the tense nuclear standoff with the West. But it is also a time for remembering wounded veterans or those who have lost loved ones.

Students' Day (November 4)

This commemorates the day in 1979 when radical students stormed the US embassy in Tehran and held more than fifty US diplomats and marines hostage for the next 444 days. In the Islamic Republic, the seizure of the embassy is still feted as a heroic revolutionary act and demonstrations are held across the country. The most important is held outside the former site of the US embassy, in downtown Tehran, where the siege took place. Thousands of students gather to chant "Death to America!" and burn effigies of Uncle Sam. Despite the hard rhetoric, any visiting foreigners are likely to be treated with benign curiosity and laughter rather than hostility.

The hostage siege was of great significance: it further radicalized the revolution and sidelined relative moderates like pragmatic prime minister Mehdi Bazargan, who was forced to resign. The seizure of the embassy caused a rupture in Tehran–Washington relations that has yet to be repaired. But many of the leading student radicals in the hostage siege went on to become reformist politicians pushing for change in the Islamic Republic.

Nuclear Energy Day (April 8)

This day feting Iran's nuclear program is a recent innovation. It marks the anniversary of Iran's achievement in enriching uranium to a sufficient degree to make nuclear fuel for atomic power plants. While Western powers have accused Tehran of seeking to produce nuclear weapons, Iran insists it only wants energy and it has defied calls for it to shelve the atomic drive.

Demonstrations are regularly held proclaiming the mantra that "Nuclear energy is Iran's undeniable right," which has become one of the country's main slogans in recent years.

chapter four

MAKING FRIENDS

FRIENDSHIP IN IRAN

Making friends as a foreigner seems extremely easy in Iran. Everywhere you go, people will want to engage you in conversation, ask you about your country, and want to know what you think of Iran. You will be showered with invitations to tea and meals and even given gifts (postcards and other souvenirs) by complete strangers. This is partly because the idea of friendship (*dusti*) is valued highly by Iranians. War and economic problems have meant that life has not been easy for many people over the last years and they have learned to count on each other. Iranians proudly say how strangers will immediately stop to help if they see a car broken down or someone in trouble. Perhaps the most important friends are within the extended family—families in Iran are usually extremely close units (see Chapter 5), who come even closer together at times of celebration (such as births) and mourning (such as deaths). It is quite a widely held view in Iran that families there are much closer and more loyal than families in the West—they could be right. Both men and women are also likely to form close bonds with classmates at school and university that last for life. These are loyalties that can also leave their mark in professional life.

While like anywhere else it pays to be streetwise, don't be distrustful of seemingly spontaneous kindness. In Iran, it is often for real, with no ulterior motive. Shopkeepers might offer sweets, an Iranian tourist might insist on buying you a postcard as a souvenir, or a fellow passenger may with a smile quietly pay your shared taxi fare.

Of course, it is one thing to make acquaintances and another to make friends. In Iran, making genuine friends as a visiting foreigner, like any other country in the world, is not always straightforward. Western visitors are likely (although not always) to be considerably richer than Iranians they meet and the question of money can always cause underlying strains. Despite the similarities to life in Europe and the United States, some aspects of Iranian culture (*farhang*) are very different and breaking this barrier takes time, understanding, and effort. As previously mentioned, Western countries have not always played the most noble role in Iran's history and this can lead to suspicion. Above all, many Iranians in the workplace are understandably bitter that foreigners on assignments earn several times as much as they do despite perhaps having similar qualifications. Foreigners working for embassies, media groups, or oil firms come and go but it is the Iranians who stay and form the backbone of the operation. A foreigner can also leave the country very quickly if necessary, an option that is not open to most Iranians. But if you succeed in overcoming these issues, a friendship made in Iran is something to be treasured and it will likely last for life.

INTERACTING WITH IRANIANS

Given the sharp words that are frequently flung between the Iranian government and the West, a visitor might expect to be regarded with suspicion

and even hostility in public. There *is* lots of anti-Western rhetoric in public in Iran—just listen to the shouts of "*Marg bar Amrika!*" (Death to America!) chanted by worshipers after Friday prayers, for example. This is sometimes extended to include "*Marg bar Englezstan!*" (Death to England—curiously, the slogan "Death to Britain!" does not exist) or whichever country is currently out of favor with the Islamic Republic. State media and the country's leaders repeatedly slam the "bullying" of Western powers and the "lies" propagated by the Western media.

But such rhetoric should not trouble foreign visitors, who should remember that it's a matter of politics, directed at governments and not at individuals. Even the people chanting these slogans would probably be delighted to engage in a political debate with a Western visitor, providing the language barrier can be overcome. Look at people's faces during an anti-Western demonstration such as the one marking the victory of the Islamic revolution and you will discover smiles rather than hostility.

For the most part, Iranians have a great curiosity toward foreign visitors. They are well-educated and well-informed and it's not unusual to be accosted by someone who wants to discuss the finer points of Western literary traditions with you. They are also not afraid of talking politics, be it about Western countries or their own.

It is refreshing to find that in modern Iran people have little fear of talking to foreigners. In theory, Iranians could be arrested for having "contacts with foreigners" but this usually refers to accusations of passing secrets to foreign embassies. In the streets at least, ordinary people are astonishingly ready to say what they think about the economy, the government, or world powers. It is interesting to see how many people, often strangers, discuss the important political questions of the day on public transportation.

MAKING CONVERSATION IN PERSIAN
Basic Phrases
Making some basic conservation in Persian will endear you to almost everyone in Iran and make you an instant celebrity. The traditional way of

saying hello is *salaam*, although some people use the full Arabic *salaam aleikom*. Depending on the time of day, you can wish someone *sobh bekheir* (good morning) or *shab bekheir* (good evening). "Yes" in Persian is *bale* (with the stress on the first syllable, as in "ballet"), though in colloquial speech *areh* is often used. "No" is *nakheir*, though in speech this is almost always shortened to *na*.

As in the Arab world, no one would even think of starting a conversation without inquiring after the other person's health. It's not normally necessary to reply; the most important thing is to make the same inquiry in return. Having got this out of the way, you can then attack the matter at hand. The normal openings for a conversation are "*Hal-e shoma?*" (How are you?) or just "*Shoma khoub-i?*" (You are fine?). You might reply "*Man khoubam*" (I'm fine) or "*Bad nistam*" (I'm not bad). It will not be long before the curious ask "*Shoma ahl-e kodoum keshvar hastid?*" (Which country are you from?) to which you might reply "*Man az Amrika hastam*" (I'm from the United States). People will likely want to know what you think of Iran, and will be delighted by a positive answer. "*Iran ra kheli dust daram*" (I love Iran) or "*Iran kheli khub-e*" (Iran's great!) is likely to bring a smile to Iranians' faces. Some may complain that the government (*dowlat*) in Britain or the United States is *bad*, or about the domestic *eghtesad* (economy).

This being Iran, personal questions will follow with surprising rapidity, especially the inevitable "*Shoma ezdevaj kardid?*" (Are you married?). It is also considered normal to ask "*Hoghug-e shoma chand-e?*" (How much are you paid?). People will also be very curious to know "*Mazhab-e shoma chi-ye?*" (What is your religion?) to which the stock answer for most Westerners will be "*Man masihi-am*" (I'm Christian). Having exhausted these possibilities, it might be time to switch to another language. The phrase "*Shoma Englisi balad-id?*" (Do you speak English?) will be useful.

The biggest obstacle in making friends is the language. Some Iranians, especially in Tehran, speak perfect English or possibly French or German. People who want to practice will inevitably latch on to you. In other situations, however, you may find people's grasp of English is rudimentary or nonexistent.

Don't Be Tired!

The most idiosyncratic of colloquial Persian phrases is *Khasteh naboshi!*, which translates as "Don't be tired!" Its use is ubiquitous. The phrase is used essentially as a greeting to anyone doing any kind of work—this could be in an office, in a restaurant, playing sports, or climbing a mountain. Of course the person addressed may be extremely tired if they have been working, but in the polite world of Iranian society this seems not to matter.

Iranians are often curious to find out what the equivalent of *Khasteh naboshi!* is in English but the simple truth is that there is no good translation for this most Persian of concepts.

A very good way to integrate socially in big cities like Tehran is to join the thousands of people from all social classes who take picnics high into the hills on a Friday. Any foreigner is likely to have numerous invitations to join a picnic or play a spot of volleyball and it's a great way to meet like-minded people—so long as you have the stamina for the steep mountain trails. Expect to be told *Khasteh naboshi*! very many times!

Conversation Topics

Many Iranians, especially men, are fanatical soccer fans, and may be better informed about the European leagues than foreign visitors. This is because most top European games are broadcast live and free to view on Iranian state television. Be prepared, if you can, to wax lyrical about the European game, say what your favorite team is, and commiserate about the fortunes of Iran's talented but perennially underperforming national side.

As mentioned above, Iranians have far fewer scruples about asking personal questions than in the West. It is relatively normal to ask how much a foreigner's salary is or how high their rent is. One of the first questions you will have to field is whether you are married. If the answer is "no" be prepared for a follow-up "*chera*?" (why?)— Iranians have a horror of staying unmarried above a certain age and cannot understand why a foreigner would want to remain single voluntarily.

Politics also looms large in conversation, be it the situation in Iran or outside. All Iranians are also happy to talk for ages about the country's attractions, be it the excellent climate, its ancient sites, or the beauty of cities outside Tehran. The congested capital's inhabitants have a great enthusiasm for the lush and rainy north (*shomal*) of the country and are not shy in recommending that foreigners should visit there.

PERSIAN NAMES

The variety and descriptiveness of many Iranian names make those used in the West seem dull by comparison. Of course, many people in Iran have Islamic or Arabic names. The most popular names for men might be Mohammad after the Prophet himself, or Ali and Hossein after his descendants. Reza, after the eighth Shiite imam, is also very popular. Many women are called Fatemeh (Fatima) after the Prophet's daughter or Massoumeh after Imam Reza's sister.

However, there is a multitude of names of Persian origin that are still frequently used in Iran. For men, many of these come from heroes of the national epic the *Shahnameh* by Ferdowsi such as Arash, Babak, or Siavash. Omid, meaning hope, is a boy's name. Sirous and Koroush are two versions of the name of Cyrus the Great. Shahab is a meteor. Some widely used names also recall biblical prophets who feature in the Koran such as Ebrahim (Abraham), Yahya (John), and Issa (Jesus).

For women, the choice of names seems even wider. If for men the main source of Persian names is the *Shahnameh*, then for women it is flowers (for example, Lili, Narguess, Nasrin, or Shaghayegh). But women may also be named after planets, ideas, or precious stones. Other popular names include Bita (unique), Forough (brightness), Zohreh (Venus), Souzan (flame), and Elham (inspiration). As a boy can be called Omid (hope), a girl may be called Arezou (wish).

On marrying, Iranian women do not take their husband's surname and keep their maiden names for the rest of their lives although of course both sons and daughters will take their father's surname.

SOCIAL CUSTOMS

Understanding the elaborate social rituals that underpin most human interactions in Iran will go a long way toward making you feel at home in society. It is also important to find a balance between respecting the Islamic rules that are the laws of the country and feeling relaxed in a modern society.

Ta'rof—When No Means Yes . . .

One of the most confusing and potentially awkward social customs for the foreign visitor is *ta'rof*—the polite rejection of something one actually wants to receive. Initially this may seem unnecessary and insincere but it is an integral part of all interactions in Iran and underlines the importance of courtesy in the culture.

You are in a taxi, for example, and at the end of the ride you offer to pay—the driver may look at you in mock horror and say "*Mehmoun-e man bash*" (Be my guest) or "*Befarmian!*" (Please!). Of course the driver has a living to make and does want your money; he is just being polite. You should insist on payment three times and on the third the driver will invariably take your money with a grateful smile.

The same principle operates in shops, restaurants, hair salons, or anywhere where money changes hands. It is important to master *ta'rof* if you are staying in Iran for any length of time. Tales abound in Tehran of foreign residents who gratefully ran off without paying when their barber or taxi driver made *ta'rof* by pretending to refuse payment. The foreigner probably left with the most wonderful picture of Iranian generosity, but the poor barber or taxi driver was left empty-handed. Iranians are hospitable but don't expect to be offered basic services for free!

Sometimes *ta'rof* can reach bizarre extremes. For example, a taxi driver in Tehran, perhaps of the more unscrupulous breed, may first refuse payment and then once you pay him tell you bluntly you have not paid enough. Then when you offer the extra sum, he will again make *ta'rof* before accepting the additional notes. It's all part of the daily ritual of Iranian life.

Curiosity

Iranians are also hugely curious (*fouzoul*). Without much preamble, they are happy to ask intimate question about salaries, love life, and rents. They love to gossip, often about other people, and the parks at weekends are filled with families and friends taking a stroll while animatedly talking. In days gone by, there was a quaint custom at New Year known as *falgoush* (fortune hearing), where people would secretly eavesdrop on strangers' conversations and use them to tell their own fortunes. The custom is said to have been particularly popular with young women wondering if the New Year would see them meet a husband. Unsurprisingly, *falgoush* is now deemed socially unacceptable and has become almost extinct.

To Handshake or Not to Handshake?

Iranian men are inveterate handshakers and you should shake hands even with close acquaintances whom you see every day. Handshakes between men and women are a more complicated issue. In theory, it is forbidden (*haram*) for people to have any bodily contact with members of the opposite sex in the Islamic Republic. Current President Mahmoud Ahmadinejad and his predecessor, Mohammad Khatami, were both attacked by the hard-line press when they were photographed making rare handshakes with women. With foreigners, however, the rules seem a little more permissive and no one will arrest you in Iran for shaking hands with a woman.

The golden rule for a Western man is let the woman take the initiative; in other words, don't create an embarrassing situation by offering your hand to a woman who does not want to shake it. However, if a more Westernized woman does offer you her hand, it would be considered petty and insulting to refuse it. Iranian women are well educated and nowadays perhaps more likely to speak a foreign language than men, given they form the majority at colleges and universities. They are articulate and opinionated about their country and male visitors should not be shy about engaging them in conversation, while respecting the culture at the same time.

A good gesture to use in any situation is to place your right hand on your heart. This can be used to mean many things: that you are touched by a gesture, that you are pleased to meet someone, or that you have enjoyed your meal but have eaten enough. It is also a very useful gesture to use when greeting a woman if it is deemed inappropriate to shake hands.

Male Dress
One thing that is not necessary in Iran is to dress up too much. Ties are generally frowned upon—although not illegal—as they are seen as a symbol of Western imperialism. Most officials generally content themselves with an open-necked shirt and jacket and will probably appreciate it if you dress in a similar way. You may see some people who work for private businesses wearing ties, but it is

still not common. Ties were popular for the upper and middle classes before the Islamic revolution and today they are still used when men want to dress up particularly well for a wedding party or major private celebration.

Dress to Impress: What Women Wear in Iran

Some foreign women do the very minimum to obey the dress laws in Iran, maybe just wearing a bandana as a head scarf and a long shirt. But whatever one's personal views, such behavior will not impress the more conservative elements and may encourage unwelcome stares from men. Foreign female visitors are better off dressing like a modern Iranian woman and this can be brought off in a way that is perfectly stylish and will make you feel much more at ease in Iranian society.

The more conservative women in Iran wear the *chador*, which literally means tent and is a single wraparound garment that envelops the body from head to toe, leaving only the face and hands visible. It's worth noting that hardly any women cover their face completely. The *chador* is not easy to wear and women frequently have to readjust the folds in the street to ensure they are properly covered. The only situation where a foreign woman might wear this garment would be in a mosque or at some other holy site. Otherwise you'd be crazy to wear it as it's not compulsory and Iranian women would simply laugh at you!

Foreigners are better off with a *manto*, a long, thin coat that goes down to the knees and does the job of obeying the dress laws while being comfortable and possibly stylish. You don't have to wear black—nowadays all manner of colors and styles are available and perfectly acceptable. The garment should not be body-hugging tight but foreigners are likely to be allowed more  leeway in these matters than native Iranians. You can easily buy a *manto* after arriving in Iran in any shopping center for little more than $10.

This of course should be topped off by the *hijab* (head scarf). Again, you will see a huge range of colors and styles on the streets. It can be tied under your chin but many Iranian women wrap shawls around their heads, which may seem more stylish. There is also the *maghanae,* a kind of ready-made *hijab* that you just throw over your head and covers

 well below the shoulders. It's normally black, dark blue, or green and worn by students and schoolchildren. A foreigner normally would not wear it but it does have the advantage of not needing to be tied or adjusted.

VISITING AN IRANIAN HOME

An invitation to an Iranian home is a great honor and is likely to be a highlight of any trip. Iranians are proud of their hospitality and will go to great lengths to look after a *mehmoun* (guest), especially a foreign one. Here you will see people relaxed and outgoing, away from the rules that prevail on the street.

It is considered polite to bring a gift: normally a box of *shirini* (sweet cakes or cookies) although if you've brought any choice tea from back home this will be appreciated even more. It goes without saying that before entering the house you should remove your shoes. You might be offered slippers but it's perfectly acceptable to walk around in socks and it's also comfortable given that most Iranian homes are covered in wonderful carpets.

Most meals will start with the first of many offers of tea. In a legacy of the cultural and

political influence Russia had on Iran in the nineteenth century, tea is brewed in a *samovar*, the traditional Russian tea urn. Water is boiled in the lower chamber and this is then added to the strong tea brewing on top. You will then be presented with a glass bowl to choose from a glistening array of fresh sweet cucumbers and tomatoes and then another bowl with fruit. (In Iran, it's perfectly normal to eat fruit before your meal.) These are normally eaten with a knife and fork from a small plate. You'll also be offered a vast array of nuts and dried fruit, so it's quite possible to fill up before the meal has even begun.

The meal proper in some households, especially more traditional ones, may be served simply on a sheet on the floor (*sofreh*), with the diners seated around with their legs crossed. Eating from this position while not putting your face in the food or dropping any on the floor proves uncomfortable for many foreigners. However, Iranian hosts are extremely sensitive to any discomfort on the part of their guests and will set up a small table if you are unable to master eating on the floor. This can be somewhat embarrassing if you are alone at a table. But in any case, better-off households, especially in Tehran, would not think of eating on the floor and take all meals seated as a group at a table.

The food will keep on coming, so make sure you have arrived hungry. There is likely to be a selection of kebabs and stews as well as a huge plate of Basmati rice. Iranians normally eat the main course with a spoon and fork, and no knife. For dessert, expect delicious Iranian cakes followed by fruit and sweets and yet more offers of tea. You will need some time to digest. Choose the right moment to leave—not too soon but also not too late as no Iranian host would dream of even dropping a hint to a guest that it's time to go. Generally, most dinner parties will start to break up around midnight.

chapter five

PRIVATE &
FAMILY LIFE

IRANIAN HOUSES AND APARTMENTS
Half a century ago, better-off Iranian families
could have expected to live in palatial bungalows
with large gardens. But the huge demographic
changes in recent years mean that this has now
changed. All but the superrich in Iranian cities
live nowadays in apartment blocks.

For low-income earners, home means a tiny flat,
but the rich may have a luxurious apartment with a
shared swimming pool, underground parking
garage, gym, and sweeping views. The last years in
Tehran especially have seen an unprecedented

construction boom. The old Qajar-era bungalows, which often had large gardens, have been mercilessly ripped down and replaced by huge towers (*borj*) that can accommodate hundreds of people. There is barely any spare ground left in leafy northern Tehran that is not being turned into a modern development.

The capital has now become an urban megalopolis with the migration from the provincial towns (*shahrestan*), creating a population of 7 million in the city and almost as many in the wider suburbs. Satellite towns like Karaj to the west have lost their distinct identities and become dormitories for workers from the capital with populations already in the millions. As a result, the face of Tehran has changed beyond all recognition and older residents will often reminisce nostalgically about how peaceful and bucolic the city was in former times,

For all Iranians, the price of property (*maskan*) has become a major problem in recent years as the move from country to city fuels a huge demand for urban dwellings. Prices for the best apartments in Tehran are already in the millions of dollars and easily comparable with those in a Western city. Even buying a modest first apartment may be out of reach for a young middle-income buyer. It has become fashionable for first-time buyers in Tehran to purchase property way out in the suburbs where it is cheaper and rent it out as an investment while continuing to live with their parents.

THE IRANIANS AT HOME

Amid all the urban difficulties created by overpopulation, Iranians keep their homes very separate from the outside. Being welcomed inside someone's house from the stressful chaos on the streets is like entering a different world. In few countries is there such a strong division between the public and private worlds, a phenomenon accentuated by the society's strict Islamic rules.

The Living Room

In almost all households, Persian carpets will be the key element of furniture. They are used for sitting on, relaxing on, and eating off (with the

addition of a protective plastic sheet). Little of the actual floor is usually visible, such is the enthusiasm for the carpet. Their use gives an Iranian home a much more spacious look than a Western apartment and it is usually free of clutter. It also means that in almost all cases guests should remove their shoes before entering the house.

This protects the carpets and is in line with the Iranian abhorrence of dirt from the street entering the home, as in any Islamic society.

Surrounding the carpet will be chairs, which is where visitors will be encouraged to sit. A small low table will usually be covered with huge bowls

of nuts and fruit, which is the absolute minimum
that is offered to any guest, along with tea. They
are normally eaten with small plates and knives.
There will be at least one sofa in almost all
houses. And of course a television, which will
invariably be kept on all day. The kitchen is the
undisputed realm of the lady of the house.

The Bathroom

Toilets in the more luxurious apartments will be
Western-style but those in less fancy places could
be of the squat kind. In any case, there is likely to
be a choice between toilet paper and the more
traditional water hose (attached to a tap next to
the toilet) for cleaning. Iranians do not worry
about spraying water all over the bathroom
during showers and ablutions and guests will
always be advised to put on a pair of plastic
sandals before entering.

Public and Private

Iran imposes strict rules on behavior in public
and there is sometimes a noticeable difference
between how relaxed people are in public and in
private. Although this was not the case in the first
years of the Islamic revolution, the authorities
nowadays generally do not interfere with what
people do in private behind closed doors. Raids
on mixed-sex parties (formally illegal) do still
take place, but with less frequency than before,
and usually because of complaints about noise
from neighbors. This means that the private

home is the place to relax and talk freely. In Iran, the best night out is considered to be attending a dinner or a party (*mehmouni*) at the home of a friend. Iranians strongly protect the privacy of their home and most apartment blocks will have closed circuit television to identify any unwelcome intruders. Apartment blocks and houses are usually protected by high walls and gates, which are for privacy as much as security.

IN THE VILLAGE

The pace and nature of life in a village is of course very different. With the migration to cities, a far smaller proportion of the population lives in the village than was the case fifty years ago. Four

generations of one family may live under the same roof in a village, with people perhaps just sleeping on the floor. In some of the best-situated villages, city dwellers have started buying up the available property. Indeed, it seems that much of north Tehran decamps each spring and summer vacation to newly built villas in villages in the north close to the Caspian Sea.

Few Iranian films evoke the atmosphere of an Iranian village as well as Darioush Mehrjui's 1969 masterpiece, *The Cow* (*Ghaav*). The story of a simple village man whose dearest love is his cow—

whose disappearance causes him to go mad—the film is an extraordinary document of a way of life that has now become increasingly rare.

POPULATION EXPLOSION

The population explosion over the last half century and the movement of people from villages to towns is one of the most significant developments in modern Iranian history. Iran's population at the start of the 1970s was less than 30 million; now it is more than 70 million. Forty years ago, the majority of people lived agrarian lives that saw them tied to their land and villages. But in recent years there has been a huge influx into the cities, especially Tehran. These demographic changes have had a massive impact on the country's social fabric, creating a huge and often poor urban population. Millions of people from the *shahrestan* have come to Tehran in search of the work and money they cannot find at home. The population growth is now stabilizing, due largely to a change of heart by the authorities in the 1990s to actively promote birth-control methods such as condoms and the pill.

MARRIAGE AND RELATIONSHIPS
Marriage

Marriage is the key event in the life of an Iranian. Iran, especially Tehran, can seem liberal compared to many Middle Eastern societies but this does not alter the fact that premarital sexual relations are banned by law and frowned upon by society. In today's tough economic times, it is also often only through marriage that young people can find the money to buy a house. As a result, Iranians tend to marry young. Many are shocked by foreigners who are still single in their thirties—in Iran this would be seen as either a calamity or an act of social defiance. The unmarried should be prepared to

expect a barrage of fascinated questions—"*Chera ezdevaj nakardid? Dir shod!*" (Why aren't you married yet? It's getting late!) Many Iranians marry in their early twenties and as the thirties approach, particularly for women, society regards them as moving past their sell-by date. But while this is the rule, it should be noted that as ever in this country there are always exceptions.

The act of choosing a spouse is also very different from in the West. In most families, it will be the parents, in particular the mother, who makes the final decision and perhaps even the selection of a spouse. Marrying in defiance of one's mother is seen as the ultimate act of anti-parental rebellion, although it does happen. Female virginity is usually considered an essential precondition for marriage.

Weddings themselves are usually the most spectacular event in an Iranian's social calendar. A gargantuan feast is prepared, with those wonderful, sophisticated dishes that feature large in Iranian cookery books but are nonexistent in restaurants. Everyone dresses up—as mentioned previously, men will often sport a tie for wedding celebrations even if they do not at any other time. The bridal dress is usually expensive and elaborate—little different, if at all, to the dresses worn by brides in the West. For the more liberal families, a wedding celebration is also a rare chance for music and dancing with friends in a public space without the threat of a police warning. While theoretically it is against the law, marriage parties often become slightly wild. A minor scandal was caused when photographs of Ali Daei, Iran's best-known soccer star, appeared showing him dancing at his wedding and his bride without a veil.

The bridal car will be topped off with a huge ribbon and flowers and likely driven up urban highways at an even more extreme speed than usual. The Iranian obsession with the video camera (no one who can afford one seems to be without it, or to leave it out of their pocket for an instant) is even more in evidence. One of the most bizarre sights of a wedding day is a man leaning precariously with most of his torso out of a speeding car on a highway in order to obtain the best possible shots of the bridal vehicle with his video camera.

Temporary Marriage (*Sigheh*)

Uniquely in Islam, Shiite Islam offers the possibility of a temporary marriage, known in Persian as *sigheh*. It is sometimes known as a "pleasure marriage," which is a fair description of its purpose. In *sigheh*, a man and woman can agree to be legally married for a limited period lasting as little as an hour. The idea is seen by its defenders as a way for genuine sexual needs to be fulfilled in a legal and proper way. Critics see it as little more than organized prostitution. A government minister in 2007 caused a storm when he suggested actively promoting *sigheh* as a way to solve the sexual problems of young people. In any case, temporary marriage is still not a widespread phenomenon in Iran (although certainly it is used) and it is not a concept that outsiders should raise without care. In theory, a man could take a second wife under a temporary marriage alongside his first lawful wife. But although polygamy is theoretically possible in Iran, in reality it is rare.

FAMILY PLANNING AND SEX

There has been a complete change in thinking about family planning in Iran in the last two decades. In the years immediately after the revolution, families were officially encouraged to have as many children as possible. The idea was to create thousands of new "little revolutionaries" who would make Iran an even more powerful country in the future. It was also seen as necessary to counter the horrifying losses of the eight-year war with Iraq. By and large people responded, resulting in a population explosion in the 1980s. But it then became clear that the economy could not sustain such a huge youth population, which was starting to suffer chronic unemployment. The Rafsanjani presidency reversed the policy, and encouraged families to have only two children.

Today, the population is still growing but at a much less sharp rate than before. President Ahmadinejad raised a number of eyebrows when he said families should produce more children to assure the country's greatness. But there seems no chance now of the state going back on its past pragmatism. The upshot of this is that condoms are readily available over the counter at pharmacies. There are even factories for home-produced condoms. The pill is also readily available. Family planning is actively promoted by the authorities in what many outsiders see as an extremely enlightened attitude, compared to the unwillingness of other states in the region to grapple with the issue. Abortion is banned in Iran, with the only exceptions allowed when the woman's life is proven to be in danger.

Attitudes toward sex are, of course, colored by the official ban on premarital sexual relations and the importance of virginity. Some Iranian youths appear very repressed. There is a rather shocking black-market trade in home videos of women in private situations, such as dressing or swimming.

Homosexuality

Homosexuality is strictly illegal in Iran.
Surprisingly, sex-change operations are not and the
state can even provide funding for people who
want to change their sex. Permission for sex-
change operations came in a *fatwa* from Ayatollah
Khomeini himself. The state sees transsexuals as
sick and in need of medical help. As a result, Iran
carries out more sex-change operations than any
other country in the world after Thailand.

The degree to which homosexuals are repressed
in Iran is difficult for a foreigner to discover and it
is a matter of huge controversy abroad. President
Ahmadinejad caused astonishment when he
declared there were "no homosexuals" in Iran.

CHILDHOOD AND ADOLESCENCE
Children

Iranians love to indulge children (*bache*). The
approach toward parenting seems a little more
permissive than in the West and children are
positively encouraged to jump around and make
noise. Western residents walking their children in
Tehran parks often find their offspring the subject
of the most lavish praise from passers-by, who
think nothing of stroking, squeezing, or touching
the child to show their goodwill. They will often
use *Mashallah*, an Arabic phrase that is invoked
when praising something beautiful to emphasize
that it comes from God and thus avoid inviting the
dangers of the "evil eye."

Education

Schooling starts from age seven with five years of elementary school, then three years at junior high school, and four years at high school. Competition for places at the best universities is ferocious, although in recent years the creation of private universities has greatly increased the number of places available.

The standard of teaching is high. But a degree is no guarantee of finding a good job and it is not hard to find over-qualified young people delivering pizzas or driving taxis. There has been a substantial brain drain to countries such as Canada that take advantage of the excellent education of Iranians. The lack of employment opportunities also puts a strain on parents, who may have to work extra hours in order to see their children through university.

For young men, military service of around two years is obligatory from the age of eighteen—how long depends on the hardship or ease of the service.

APPEARANCE AND PLASTIC SURGERY

Iran's youth, both male and female, take great care of their appearance. Many young men would not think of stepping out without sporting carefully gelled and styled hair, and with some women the same is true for makeup. One surprise for visitors to urban Iran is the number of young people walking around with plasters stuck across their noses. The explanation: there is a tremendous fashion for nose jobs (*damagh amali*), especially among women but also among men, and across all social classes.

TIME OUT

Given the amount of traffic on weekend nights in Tehran, it seems that everyone is up to something. Iranians take their leisure seriously, and have a reasonable amount of time to enjoy it in. The weekend in Iran is Thursday and Friday: everyone has Friday off and most offices are shut on Thursdays as well. People also have a fair amount of holiday time; most long vacations are taken at the New Year in March and in late summer in August. The number of national holidays in the country adds further days off.

In general, Iranians enjoy being together in groups. As in many Middle Eastern countries, there is a fear of being alone and being seen to be alone. Iranians are a gregarious people and whether hiking up a mountain or enjoying a kebab in a restaurant, they like to be part of a large group.

Unsurprisingly in this diverse country, the manner in which people enjoy their leisure varies considerably. Before the revolution, Tehran was seen as the playground of the Middle East, complete with casinos and cabarets. These have now gone, and people focus their social lives on parties and dinners in private homes. The complexity of Iranian dishes means that cooking can easily fill a lot of free time. Soccer is a national obsession, although other sports are also popular.

EATING

Iranian food is acknowledged as one of the great cuisines of the world and Iranians are justly proud of it. But as in many countries, the best place to sample real Iranian food is at a private home and not in a restaurant. Often it is only in a house that visitors will be able to enjoy the full range of regional and national dishes and understand the elaborate culture behind them.

Eating at Home

Starters

An Iranian meal is likely to start with *sabzi* (herbs), fresh herbs possibly with walnuts, and feta cheese with bread. Eating the herbs is said to build up your appetite for the meal ahead. A standard soup is *ab-e jo*, barley soup. There is also a thick meat soup known as *ash*, which is popular  for breaking the *Ramazan* fast but simply too heavy and rich to be considered a starter. Another popular starter is the attractively named *koukou*, an omelet with a passing resemblance to a Spanish tortilla that is often served cold. Olives (*zeytun*) may also be served but do not expect the endless Arab-style sequence of *mezze* starters, which are not really part of Iranian cuisine.

Main Dishes

The main meal is likely to include delicious kebabs with rice, the standard Iranian dish. Forget the slices of indefinable meat served up after a late night out in the West: Iranian kebabs are the real thing, meat cooked on skewers over a charcoal fire. Often they will be cooked in the open over a barbecue—this is the one time an Iranian man can be seen helping out with cooking, sweating as he fans the coals. There are many kinds of kebabs— the most basic is *kubide* (minced), *juje* is chicken, while the best of all is *barg* (lamb). These are always served with rice (*berenj*). Iranians are justifiably proud of their rice, which is always of the Basmati kind. It is cooked and sifted several times so the final product is steaming hot and feather light. It will be topped off by a circle of saffron-colored rice and butter. Many Iranians will munch their way through an entire raw onion while eating their meat. Rice is often served with barberries (*zereshk*), which provide a beautiful sweet-sour taste.

The meal will also include beef or lamb stews (*khoresht*), one of the jewels of Iranian cuisine, and the perfect complement to the rice. Traditional stews include *gheimeh bademjoun* (eggplant stew) and *ghormeh sabzi*, which is made with several different herbs. But the greatest of them all is *fesenjun*, a rich and original creation made with chicken, pomegranates, and walnuts. Other

delicacies are *kofte tabrizi*, gigantic tennis-ball-sized meatballs from the north of Iran often stuffed with dates and served in a rich sauce. *Khashke bademjoun* is a smoky eggplant puree. As elsewhere in the Middle East, stuffed vegetables (*dolme*) are also popular.

A feature of Iranian cuisine from medieval times to the present day is the use of sweet ingredients such as apricots, berries, oranges, and apples in savory main dishes. Perhaps the greatest Iranian dish of all is jeweled rice (*morasa polo*), which is served with carrots, crystallized sugar, saffron, orange, and dried fruit. This dish, which looks as extraordinary as it tastes, is nowadays only brought out on the most special occasions such as weddings.

Dessert
After all this, you may not have enough room for dessert, which normally includes Iranian cakes and cookies. The former can be a bit too creamy for some Western tastes—although slim locals seem to gorge themselves endlessly. The cookies are delicious, often flavored with saffron and varying greatly from region to region.

It is now time to thank your host—Iranian cuisine is time-consuming and elaborate. Even preparing the rice to ensure it has just the correct light texture can take hours. For a major feast, the host may have been preparing the dishes for days.

Eating Out
Restaurants

Most Iranians rarely step inside a restaurant, the idea being why pay for something you can get free and better at home! Often, an Iranian restaurant will offer only a limited selection of dishes, most likely kebabs. Standards of hygiene are generally good and the quality is fine, but an endless diet of kebabs can become quite dull. Service can be offhand and the plastic tablecloths, elevator music, and bread in plastic bags are often uninspiring. Not all Iranian restaurants are like this: a popular venue with locals is the *restoran-e sonati* (traditional restaurant), a themed restaurant where the food tends to be more interesting and waiters in traditional dress serve up regional specialties. Iranian food is rarely expensive: a plate of kebabs and rice usually costs little more than US $5.

In Tehran, international food is increasingly popular with the moneyed elite. There are several good Indian, Chinese, Italian, Lebanese, and French restaurants. However, they are often hidden in the basements of hotels or shopping centers and are hard to find at random. A three-course international meal in Tehran with (soft) drinks is likely to cost around US $20 per person.

Fast Food

Cheaper ideas include the increasingly ubiquitous fast-food restaurants, which are a known haunt of flirting couples, who seem attracted more by the social interaction than the often uninspired food. Nevertheless the atmosphere is extremely friendly and the burgers and pizzas pass muster in an Iranian kind of way. The Tehran equivalent of McDonalds is the amusingly named Boof, which is constantly opening new outlets. Fast food in Iran, however, may not be that fast—you line up to place an order, pay, and are then given a number that is finally read out over a microphone when the food is ready. Another option is the traditional kebab house, where the meat is excellent and is eaten with fresh round *taftoon* bread baked on the premises. A plate of kebabs and fresh herbs here can cost as little as US $3.

For a breakfast out, a dubious delicacy is the *kalleh pacheh* (head and legs of a sheep). The restaurants offering this are clean, cheap, and friendly. They normally also bake *taftoon* on the premises. But the food—sheep's eyes, tongue, stomach, head, legs, and whatever else—served with a bowl of the cooking juices may not be to everyone's taste.

"Hot" and "Cold" Food

In another legacy of ancient times, the idea of "hot" (*garm*) and "cold" (*sard*) foods remains important in Iranian cooking today. This does not refer to the temperature of the food but to its influence on the mood and digestion. Iranians are convinced of the

BREAD

Iranian bread is unique to the country—it is simply not possible to find the same kinds of bread anywhere else in the world. Iranians take bread very seriously and will refuse to eat it when it is not fresh.

There are four main types of bread in Iran and plenty of debate among Iranians over which is best. Bread generally acts as a culinary hoover—it is used to scoop up meat, cheese, and salad in morsel packages. Part of the fun is buying it. Bread shops sell only one of the four main types: for a different bread you have to go to a different shop. All bread is sold fresh from the oven; storekeepers would not sell anything else. In any case, if you wait too long before eating the bread or storing it, it becomes so crisp as to be inedible. Bakers usually only bake at mealtimes, three times a day, and there are long lines as breakfast, lunch, or dinner approaches. This is because subsidies mean that bread is kept cheap and it is the main carbohydrate for the poor. Despite the frustrations of standing in line, catching the whiff of the freshly baked bread early on a crisp sunny morning is one of the great simple pleasures of Iran.

In Tehran and other big cities, it is also possible to find shops making European-style bread and baguettes.

The four main types of bread are as follows:

Lavash: The most basic bread, ultra-thin layers used for scooping up food. A family will need to buy a dozen layers for a meal. It is seen by some as the poor man's bread.

Taftoon: An oval or round bread the size of a tray. Baking in a hot oven produces its characteristic air bubble dimples. It is especially good for eating with kebabs and best eaten hot.

Babari: An oblong-shaped bread with a doughy crust and a crispy inside, often topped with sesame seeds. It is very tasty with herbs or cheese.

Sangkak: The undisputed king of Iranian breads, this is a long sheet of bread of medium thickness cooked over stones or olive stones (hence its name: *sang* means stone). Lines for this bread are always the longest. It is bliss if eaten fresh but has the texture of an old carpet if stale. Watch out for any lingering small stones remaining inside the bread, but at least they prove it's genuine!

importance of having a good balance between "hot" and "cold" foods. The notion goes back to ancient Greek and Zoroastrian medicine, where it was believed that excessive "hot" food could make people hyperactive and feverish while too much "cold" food would lead to shivering and depression. Conversely, "hot" or "cold" foods could be prescribed to correct a range of ills.

The classification of hot and cold foods can seem confusing to outsiders. But generally, "hot" foods include the most widely eaten meats in Iran (lamb and chicken) and some spices, while "cold" foods include yogurt, rice, and most vegetables. Thus "hot" meat is balanced with "cold" rice and perhaps yogurt. Many Iranians remain passionately convinced of the importance of balancing the two kinds of foods, to ensure the taste is good, the digestion is smooth, and the mood temperate. They will warn of the dangers of having the wrong balance and also use the system to cure illness.

DRINKING

Alcohol is banned in Iran, but there are plenty of other options. Beer *is* available, but of course it is zero percent. The most popular Iranian brand is Delster, which is flavored with apple or lemon and is extremely refreshing on a hot day. Some would say it tastes absolutely nothing like beer. For a more beery taste, opt for imported foreign brands like Tuborg, Bavaria, and Baltika, which have good-quality zero percent options. Visitors should not be excited by mentions of "champagne" on upscale hotel menus as this will be sparkling grape juice. It is of course possible to source alcohol on the black market—smuggled in through Iraqi Kurdistan or Turkey.

Iranians are obsessive tea drinkers. The traditional way to drink tea in Iran is through a piece (*gand*) of sugar clenched between the teeth, complete with a loud sucking noise—not for those who care for their dental health. Many Iranians take their first sips of tea by pouring the liquid into a saucer and then tipping it into their mouth. Tea is always served very strong and will taste very bitter without sugar. If you want a weak cup, ask for *kam-e rang* (literally, little color). Don't think of asking for milk except in five-star hotels—the locals will think you're nuts. Coffee is not massively popular—though perhaps a little more so in the north—and you are more likely to find instant than the traditional "Turkish" style.

Cafés in the European sense are disappointingly thin in Iran—the idea of people watching over a cup of coffee does not exist. There are traditional tea houses (confusingly named *ghavekhune*, coffeehouse), where you can lounge on a divan smoking a water pipe. Such places are often wonderfully atmospheric and a good place to chat with the older generation. Increasingly popular with the young in Tehran and other major cities are coffee shops. Often tiny and extremely intimate establishments, they sell real coffee and cakes. This is where the trendy set is likely to hang out, hunched over tables in deep and hushed conversation with their partners. Indeed, going to such a coffee shop will be the focal point of a night out for many young people in Iran.

> ### TIPPING
>
> Tipping is nowhere near as widespread in Iran as in some other countries in the region. For short taxi journeys, cheaper restaurants, or hotels, tipping is absolutely not required unless you want to show great personal appreciation. In smarter restaurants, there may be a doorman to usher you in who will expect to be tipped half a dollar or so.
>
> The main season for tipping comes just ahead of the New Year, when it is customary to give employees or workers an *eidi* (festive gift). For workers in companies, this normally means a salary for a thirteenth month. But house cleaners, drivers, or cooks will also expect to be paid the equivalent of an extra month's wage as well.

PAYING

Iran's economy runs on cash. The US trade embargo means that international credit cards and traveler's checks from any company are next to useless here. As a result, the vast majority of transactions, even for

high-denomination goods, are made in cash. Until quite recently, the only note of real value was the 10,000 rial (known as a *sabzi*, or "green," because of its color and worth about US $1), meaning that many payments involved handing over huge bricks of cash. Things have improved somewhat recently with the introduction of 20,000- and 50,000-rial notes, the latter bearing a motif in support of the Iranian nuclear program.

Another innovation are "Iran checks," essentially a domestic traveler's check worth around 1 million rials (approx. US $100). They can be bought from almost any bank and are increasingly popular as a way to avoid carrying heavy wads of notes. There may be rare occasions when a credit card can be used, for example when buying a tour or a carpet from a firm that can use a payment system in Europe or the United States.

Toman or Rial?

In Iran, things are not always what they seem at first and, confusingly, this is the case with money. The national currency is the rial; in 2008 there were around 10,000 rials to the US dollar. The snag is that almost everyone, from financial bosses to shopkeepers, talks about money in terms of "tomans," which is the same as the rial but with one zero lopped off. So 10,000 rials is the same as 1,000 tomans, and if a taxi driver asks you for "5,000" at the end of a ride, he means he wants 5,000 tomans and thus 50,000 rials. The confusion means that most foreigners will end up underpaying by a factor of 10 at some point in their visit—but of course the Iranian vendor can be counted on to point out the error, as always in the most polite way possible!

SPORTS
Watching and Supporting
Soccer

Like almost everywhere else in the world, soccer (*footbol*) is the number one spectator sport with Iranians. Expect most men and quite a large number of women to be watching their televisions or at least listening to the radio each time the national side plays an important match, with fervent celebrations of car-honking and flag-waving greeting a victory. Unfortunately, the national side has not had much to fete in recent years after a humiliating first-round exit in the 2006 World Cup, and their proudest recent exploit is the legendary defeat of the archfoe the United States in the 1998 World Cup.

Just as apparent is fervent support for local clubs. Tehran supporters are split down the middle over their devotion to either of the capital's two top teams—Persepolis (named after the famed ancient site in the south) and Esteghlal (Independence). Local derbies are massive events, with around 100,000 people packed into the Azadi (Freedom) Stadium in Tehran. The atmosphere is intimidating and the noise overwhelming—an extraordinary Iranian experience. The city for once becomes eerily quiet when the two teams play as Tehranis cluster in front of their television and radio sets.

Also distinctive is the lack of women in the stadium: they are banned from attending soccer matches in Iran, on the grounds that the often raucous behavior of the male fans would be dangerous and offensive for them. Jafar Panahi's prize-winning film *Offside* (2006) chronicles the attempts of an Iranian girl to smuggle herself into the decisive World Cup qualifier against Bahrain in 2005, disguised as a man. It was banned in Iran.

A surprise attempt by President Ahmadinejad to overturn the "men only" rule in 2005 was vetoed by supreme leader Ayatollah Khamenei. A foreign female visitor will probably be allowed in to a game but may find herself ushered into the VIP box at Azadi for "security" reasons.

Other Sports

Wrestling has a big following in the country and Iran has provided many Olympic and world champions. Basketball is also a major spectator sport and players have even been shipped in from the United States to play in the Iranian league. Handball is also popular with spectators.

Zurkhaneh

Perhaps Iran's most intriguing sport for foreign spectators is *Zurkhaneh* (House of Strength). The sport consists of several disciplines, including traditional wrestling, lifting clubs and shields, and spinning in a circle at a dizzying speed. This spellbinding combination of wrestling,

weightlifting, and traditional strongman events is accompanied by traditional music and provides one of the best possible insights into the Iranian psyche. There are clubs in most Iranian cities: they can be found by asking around and visitors are usually welcome. The sport is also known as *varzesh-e bastani* (ancient sport) and Iranians are proud that its origins go back to the pre-Islamic period. Today of course religious devotion also plays its role in the sport, with the players calling on the prophets before performing their disciplines.

Sports Stars
Iran has some big soccer stars who are household names such as Ali Daei (world soccer's all-time top goal scorer); in 2008 he became the national team coach. Another big name is Hadi Saei, who won Olympic Gold in Taekwondo in 2004 and is now a reformist politician, sitting on Tehran's city council. But the greatest champion of them all is the man mountain Hossein Rezazadeh, the double Olympic champion in weightlifting's heavyweight class. His gigantic frame is ever-present in television profiles or endorsing products. A devout Muslim, Rezazadeh is famous for shouting a prayer before every lift and having the name of Abol Fazl, the brother of Imam Hossein, emblazoned on his vest.

Taking Part
It is surprisingly easy to find sporting activities in Iran. Almost everything is available—even darts and cricket—and the standard of facilities is

good. Ask an Iranian to phone the appropriate
sports federation for more information.

Women in Sports
Women are increasingly well catered to in sports
in Iran. In the years immediately after the Islamic
revolution, women's sports were frowned upon,
but since the early 1990s the situation has
improved considerably. Faezeh, the daughter of
the then President Rafsanjani, was herself a keen
sportswoman and fought hard for greater
sporting opportunities for women. Initially,
women were only encouraged to take part in
more stationary activities like shooting and
archery. But with time, they are now able to enjoy
a full range of sports including highly physical
activities like rowing, karate, canoeing, tennis, and
even rugby. One thing that has not changed,
however, is sexual segregation—women and men
have to work out at different times at sports clubs.
It would be inconceivable for women and men to
compete together in any kind of sport, in public
at least. Women also have to adhere fully to the
Islamic dress code if they are playing sports while
male spectators, coaches, or referees are in
attendance.

Park Sports
Among people in search of less formal sporting
activities, badminton is all the rage. Go to any
park on a Friday or a summer evening and all the
open spaces will be crammed with people, men

and women, pinging a shuttlecock back and forth. If you bring along a racket, you are bound to be asked to join in—a great way to make new friends. There is also plenty of informal park volleyball, although this probably requires some previous experience and skill to be truly satisfying.

Mountain Sports

Another active pursuit popular all over Iran (for both sexes) is hiking. Iran is the most mountainous country in the Middle East and in no other country in the region is hiking so popular. Iran has produced some world-class mountaineers who have climbed all the world's major peaks. There are also excellent bolted climbing routes within easy reach of Tehran and other cities. But mountain walking is also extremely popular with the

public—every Friday, the main mountain trails above Tehran are packed with locals enjoying the better air and weekend exercise. People come from all social backgrounds—fit septuagenarians, *chador*-clad women, and young children bound up the hills— perhaps the only chance they have all week for activity and decent air. The sound of a man singing poetry as he ascends a mountain is another of those unique Iranian experiences. The trails are so busy on a Friday that the walking can be a bit stressful and it might be better to choose any other day in the week.

With the help of a guide, visitors can find plenty of great treks in the Alborz Mountains around Tehran or in the Zagros Range to the west. The country as a whole has a huge choice of mountain landscapes largely unexplored by foreigners. Any mountaineer in Iran wants to ascend its highest peak, Mount Damavand. Although close to Tehran, a guided climb to the summit and back down takes the best part of a week—a feat well within the reach of a fit walker in summer although best left to alpine specialists in the winter.

CULTURE
Cinema
Iranian cinema is rightly famed worldwide for its quality and has a proud tradition dating back to well before the Islamic revolution to the dawn of the medium. Many Iranian films have won top prizes at international film festivals in recent years. Iran's best-known director in the West is probably Abbas Kiarostami, whose simple, slightly mystic fables have won him an admiring following. His *The Taste of Cherry* (*Ta'm-e Gilas*, 1997), about a man trying to commit suicide in Tehran, won the Palme d'Or in Cannes and caused much controversy back home for its

subject matter . . . and for the kiss the director received from the actress presenting the award.

But Kiarostami is only one of many very fine Iranian directors to watch out for. Others include Jafar Panahi, whose best film is the poleaxing *The Circle* (*Dayereh*, 2000), a gritty look at the problems of a group of women in Tehran that took top prize at the Venice Film Festival. Ebrahim Hatami-Kia is one of the most successful of a group of directors who specialize in making films about the 1980–88 Iran–Iraq war. A leading female director is Rakhshan Bani Etemad, who has been unafraid to tackle social issues head-on. Iran also has a horde of famous actresses and actors (such as Ezatollah Entezami, the star of *The Cow*), some of whose careers date back to before the revolution and are venerated as national treasures.

Whether this proud cinematic tradition means a visitor will ever go to the cinema in Iran is another matter. Rather than the art-house fare that is so successful in the West, many of the films screened in Iran tend to be macho shoot-em-ups or banal boy-meets-girl tales. Moreover, many of the most daring films are banned by cultural censors before they ever hit the screens and are only ever viewed in cinemas in the West. Kiarostami's 2002 film *Ten* (*Dah*) was banned in Iran, as were most of Panahi's recent efforts and a string of other high-profile pictures. It is difficult for many directors to reconcile their artistic ambitions with the strict Islamic and political rules that must be obeyed.

Unsurprisingly, plenty of business is done in pirate DVDs, whose sellers will happily flog copies of otherwise banned material for little more than US $2. They ply their trade outdoors near major squares despite occasional police crackdowns.

Music
Traditional and Western Classical

Iran's music scene is also the subject of strict rules but is nevertheless surprisingly diverse. Traditional Iranian music normally involves a small group of instrumentalists accompanying a vocalist singing traditional poetry. The songs take their time to build up to an intense climax and are not really easy listening but can be a profoundly moving experience. The undisputed master of traditional Iranian singing is Mohammad Reza Shajarian, a household name in Iran, whose rare concerts both at home and abroad sell out almost instantly. He is known in Iran simply as *ostad*—the master.

The most common instruments are the *tar* (long-necked lute), the *kamancheh* (spike fiddle, played with a bow), the *ney* (flute), and the *tombak* (drum). Some traditional concerts take place in Tehran, although not as

many as people would like. Frustratingly, any advertising tends to be by word of mouth. A likely venue to ask is the cultural center of Niavaran Palace in northern Tehran. The atmosphere of Iranians enjoying the rare event of attending a concert can be electric.

Western classical music exists in Iran and Tehran has its own symphony orchestra, whose eclectic repertoire includes Mozart as well as Iranian and Eastern composers. Western classical music was frowned upon immediately after the revolution (perhaps in response to its promotion by the deposed shah's wife) but this now seems to have changed.

Pop Music
Rock music exists in two forms—legal and illegal. Several pop bands operate freely with official permission from the Ministry of Culture and

Islamic Guidance, which deems them to be acceptable. Iran's first aboveground post-revolution pop group was Arian, which gave its first public performance in 1998 after President Khatami came to power. It was also remarkable for having female backing vocalists and instrumentalists. The band's peppy tunes are quite uplifting and they are now working on a collaboration with Irish singer Chris de Burgh.

Only a few bands win the all-important official approval, leaving a substantial underground music scene. These can range from small-scale ensembles to something more serious and any concerts they give can be subject to raids by the police. There is also a thriving Persian diaspora music scene based around Los Angeles—plenty of the music heard in Tehran traffic jams will have been produced in LA.

Art
Art galleries of modern works are surprisingly plentiful in Tehran and have a fashionable ambience. There are many talented Iranian artists—Kiarostami himself is one. Unbeknownst to many, Iran also has a spectacular collection of European art, including major works by Bacon, Picasso, Pollock, and Renoir. Built up under the deposed shah, it is now kept firmly under lock and key in Tehran's Museum of Contemporary Art and shown only to specialist visitors. Under Khatami, a large chunk was shown to the public briefly for the first time since the revolution.

chapter seven

TRAVEL, HEALTH, & SAFETY

There are many ways to travel around Iran and in its cities, from the most luxurious private train compartment to a cramped old bus. The country has a comprehensive national travel network, with most major centers connected by bus, train, and plane. Public transportation is often more difficult to use, with the metro system and buses, especially in Tehran, too busy for comfort. It may be necessary to give up concepts of personal space in these situations but women often have a better deal owing to sex segregation, which leaves their sections less busy.

ARRIVING IN IRAN
Air Travel
Virtually all international flights for Tehran leave from and land at the new Imam Khomeini International Airport (IKIA). The airport has had a difficult history—when it first opened it was shunned by many airlines amid concerns about the runway safety. It was also stormed by the Revolutionary Guards and closed down just hours after opening in May 2004 on "security" grounds,

but actually to prevent a Turkish firm operating the airport. It is now run by an Iranian state-owned operator. But using the shiny IKIA is now a relatively pleasant experience. It is also one of the few places in Tehran where it is possible to buy a proper espresso. The concourse is always crammed—whenever an Iranian goes abroad for any period of time, the whole family usually shows up for what is often an emotional farewell. The same goes for the homecoming, complete with tears and flowers.

Visa requirements vary greatly from nation to nation and embassy to embassy, but visa and passport checks are usually very smooth and as long as all is in order, visitors will be through in

minutes. Foreigners are often waved through customs. Under no circumstances should you be tempted to import alcohol into Iran as this will be picked up by the security machines that scan all luggage.

The main problem with IKIA is its distance from Tehran—stuck out in the desert, it is a 30 mile (50 km) drive and takes an hour even in the traffic-free dead of night (which is thankfully when most international flights leave; at other times, just getting out of Tehran city can take an hour). There is as yet zero public transportation to and from the airport although there is usually a good supply of taxis that will be only too happy to oblige the disembarking foreigner. However, this caused major problems during heavy snowfalls in 2008, when many passengers were left stranded at the airport for days.

Modern international airports have also been built in Mashhad and Tabriz and there are regular direct international flights (from the Arab world to Mashhad and from Turkey to Tabriz).

Train and Bus
It is possible to travel to Tehran from Istanbul by train on the once-weekly service via Tabriz and Van on Iran's only rail link to Europe. There are bus services to Tehran from Turkey as well as to neighboring Armenia.

INTERCITY TRAVEL
Bus and Taxi
Traveling by bus in Iran is normally a relatively comfortable experience, although not as leisurely as that in neighboring Turkey. The distances are in any case often very long (for example, around 18 hours from Tehran to Kerman) and in many cases it is better to take the plane. The best buses tend to be new Volvos or Scanias, while Mercedes models seem to have emerged from a 1960s time warp and are far less comfortable. It is always worth checking which make of bus is departing before booking

the ticket. Bus stations, especially in Tehran, tend to be places of organized chaos, which seem intimidating at first but generally work efficiently. There are very many bus companies but just asking around at the bus station will lead you rapidly toward the firm with the first bus leaving for your destination. Ticket prices are extremely low. A Western man should not sit next to an unmarried Iranian woman but no one will ask Western couples whether they are married. Drivers are generally professional and on the better class of services you will be offered soft drinks and snacks en route.

However, Iran has one of the world's very worst safety records on its roads, which claim around four thousand lives a year. The reason is partly the erratic driving of many Iranians, in particular the drivers of heavy goods vehicles, some of whom are at the wheel suffering from extreme exhaustion or even under the influence of drugs. Each year there are several horrific crashes involving buses, usually at night.

Travelers in southeast Iran are well advised to keep a close eye on their baggage: this is prime drug-smuggling territory and the police are likely to carry out spot checks on passing traffic.

For shorter journeys of up to three hours, shared taxis are usually available; they leave when full and charge a fixed fee. Journey times are shorter than for the bus, but stress levels will be higher as the drivers do not hang around.

Train

Iran's extensive train network is often overlooked by foreigners but it is perhaps the safest and most comfortable way to travel around the country. Premium compartments with every imaginable mobile luxury can be booked on the flagship trains to big cities like Mashhad and Tabriz, but even here prices are low. Other routes may be less well equipped but standards on overnight journeys are normally acceptable, so long as you have booked a compartment in a sleeper.

One curious fact about traveling by overnight train in Iran is that compartments are not segregated by sex (although women can ask to be placed in a compartment exclusively for women). This means you could find yourself sleeping directly opposite a member of the opposite sex—slightly odd in a country where contact between male and female strangers is so restricted. But Iranians see nothing abnormal in this. Generally, all the men will exit the compartment while the women prepare for bed.

Trains are particularly oversubscribed during Iranian New Year, when services are often booked out months in advance.

Air Travel

Iran's civilian aviation industry has the worst imaginable reputation but one that is not always justified. True, Iran has to cope with tough US sanctions, which prevent it from buying any new Boeing or Airbus aircraft. Resourcing spare parts is also a major problem. Watching the planes land at Mehrabad Airport in central Tehran, from where all domestic flights leave, can seem like traveling in time as various Soviet-made Iranian aircraft with gigantic propellers touch down. There have been several deadly crashes over the last three decades.

But it is wrong to be too alarmist. Industry employees are skilled and highly practiced in the art of keeping planes in the air despite the sanctions. The number of crashes has fallen greatly in the last decade. Generally, the system works, although there are occasional delays due to technical problems. Iran has been able to buy relatively new Airbuses secondhand from friendly states like Turkey and also has a number of Dutch Fokker jets. It is worth inquiring when booking what type of plane will be departing—the travel agent can say. Many Iranians always choose an Airbus, Boeing, or Fokker over a more ancient Soviet Tupolev for extra comfort and security. In any case, statistically the risks of flying in Iran are negligible compared to those of traveling by road.

URBAN TRAVEL
Tehran Traffic

Traffic (*terrafik*) dominates almost every conversation in Tehran. It is not just bad, it is abominable, even by the standards of the Middle East. A poorly judged journey can result in being stuck in traffic snarls for literally hours, breathing in masses of polluted air as well. Tehran has an impressive network of four-lane highways but even these are not enough to absorb the millions of cars on the city's roads. There appear to be three main reasons for this: the pricing of gasoline at the equivalent of around 10 US cents a liter (less than the price of a liter of mineral water), the lack of quality public transportation, and many young Iranians' love of driving aimlessly around the city in the evening. There was hope that a 2007 move to ration gas would improve matters, but most Tehran drivers have now learned ways to circumvent this. Listening to radio traffic reports in the rush hour can be amusing, as the presenter announces that the traffic on almost every highway in the capital is *sangin* (heavy).

Pollution

The pollution (*aludegi*) in the city is generated almost entirely by the car exhaust fumes. Some say that living in the capital is the equivalent of smoking a dozen cigarettes a day. Tehran's attractive situation—at a high altitude and surrounded by mountains—is also its curse, especially in winter when huge amounts of smog build up in the city center. During the very worst periods—generally in winter after many days of no wind—the authorities even advise people to stay at home or shut down schools. Stuck in a traffic jam, the bitter smell of carbon monoxide is palpable. The sheer volume of traffic is not the only reason for this—the make of cars is also to blame. Until recently, the bulk of cars on Iranian roads were locally manufactured Pakyans ("arrow" in Farsi), an extraordinarily inefficient vehicle that burns the same amount of fuel as a sports car and was modeled on the British Hillman Hunter, a family car of the 1960s and '70s. Like an East German Trabant, the Paykan has a certain nostalgia value but its environmental impact has been catastrophic.

Iran has now finally stopped production of these cars in favor of more modern vehicles and the affluence of middle-class Tehranis means that there is a surprising number of smart new cars on the roads. But there are plenty of Paykans still around.

Coping with Tehran Traffic

The key to ensuring that traffic doesn't ruin your day's plans is good planning and timing. In Tehran, the traffic builds up from 7:00 a.m. as schools start and it reaches a crescendo at round 8:45 a.m. with commuters. Relative calm then prevails for a few hours, before school ends and the lunch break causes brief but extremely heavy traffic for an hour after midday. But the worst is yet to come: many employees seem to leave their work exactly at 5:00 p.m., resulting in horrendous problems from that time on. The main roads from Tehran city center to the richer residential areas in the north are filled with traffic until around 7:30 p.m., by which time it is normally safe to venture outside again.

Traffic in Other Iranian Cities

Traffic in other Iranian cities cannot compare to
that in Tehran. But much of the above also applies
to the large cities of Tabriz and Mashhad, which
can become very congested in rush hour periods
and on Thursday nights.

Taxis

Most foreigners, and many Iranians, will use only
taxis for their journeys in Tehran and other big
cities. These will either normally be the Paykan or
its more congenial replacement, the Samand.
There are two types of taxi in Iran: a *savari*
(shared) or a *dar bast* (literally, door closed). The
former are basically shared cabs; as they come by
the curb they honk and you yell your destination
to the driver, who will either stop to take you or
carry on driving if he is not interested. At busy
times, dozens of Iranians stand at intersections

waiting for *savari* taxis.
Prices are very low, just
50 US cents for
traversing half of Tehran.
The unspoken code was
always that unrelated
members of the opposite
sex should avoid sitting
next to each other,
sometimes resulting in a roadside ballet as new
passengers got in and the remaining ones changed
their configuration. But things are more relaxed
these days and the code is not always observed.

But given that the process of hailing a *savari* taxi can be daunting, many will prefer to pay extra for a private taxi, or *dah bast*. Essentially, any empty car can be taken this way so long as the driver agrees on the destination or price. For a journey from north to central Tehran the price is still low, at around $4. Official taxis are marked by a horizontal stripe over the body of the car although many taxis operate unofficially as well. The other option is to take a telephone taxi (*ajans*). There are usually several *ajans* offices in most neighborhoods in Iranian cities, providing an important source of income for men who would not otherwise find work. At busy times they may have no cars, but normally there is a decent supply.

Whatever kind of taxi you take, you may be in for an interesting experience: many of the older drivers are highly educated and opinionated and may even speak some English. With a younger driver, expect to be deafened by a succession of tracks of Iranian pop on the car stereo. Incongruously, some of the most beaten-up Paykans have been lovingly fitted out with state-of-the art stereos.

A recent innovation of the Tehran municipality is a taxi service driven by, and exclusively for, women. The idea is to allow women to travel more safely. The Web site is www.womentaxi.ir.

Metro and Bus
Tehran has its own metro system, which finally opened in 1999 after years of planning dating back to before the revolution. Unsurprisingly, it is very

busy. Not all the planned lines are complete and it does not yet extend to north Tehran. But it can be useful for traveling round south Tehran, especially to the bazaar. Women have quieter carriages reserved for them, but men have to squeeze into extremely tightly packed carriages.

There is also a comprehensive bus network but it is very busy and has to cope with the city's dreadful traffic.

Driving

Long-term foreign residents in Iran usually purchase a private car with good air-conditioning to avoid the pollution. However, it takes some time to adapt to the aggressive Iranian driving style. Indeed, what passes for cautious, sensible driving in the West can be dangerous in Tehran as no one expects people to drive like this. If you have an accident, you should not leave the scene until the police arrive. Iran is one of the few countries in the Middle East where the police actively enforce the law that seat belts must be worn in the front, and they will stop vehicles that disobey this on highways.

Pedestrians

For many visitors, traffic will be their most negative experience of Tehran. Perhaps the worst-off of all are pedestrians, who have to gulp in all the pollution and risk their lives when crossing the road. The sheer volume of traffic means pedestrians have to take one lane of cars at a time, often leaving them stranded in the middle of the road as vehicles zip by on each side. Iranians are in a hurry when they are in their

cars, so do not expect the normal rules of hospitality toward foreigners to apply here!

A particular danger is the thousands of motorbikes that appear to hold the Tehran economy together by performing errands and deliveries. They can be found going the right way, going the wrong way, and on the pavement and can zoom out of nowhere without the slightest warning. For the super brave, there is always the possibility of hailing one of these bikes as a taxi. Motorbike taxis weave in and out of the traffic so journey times are much shorter. But riding pillion behind a manic driver may not be to everyone's taste . . . though some foreigners may be happy to find it possible to have so much exhilaration so cheaply!

WHERE TO STAY
Hotels in Iran run from dormitories offering beds from a dollar a night to multistar hotels where a night's rest can prove very expensive for foreigners. At the lowest end of the scale is the *mosaferkhane* (guesthouse) where bedrooms are shared by up to a dozen people (and, of course, sex-segregated). They are very cheap but may refuse to accept foreigners

altogether. A night at a one- or two-star hotel is unlikely to cost more than US $20 and could even include a breakfast of bread, eggs, and jam. Hygiene generally in Iran is not bad but hotel standards can vary greatly from place to place. There are a growing number of boutique hotels, often ambitious and worthy projects that use restored buildings that are often of great architectural interest. This is a nascent industry, but where such hotels exist they are often the best

places to stay in Iran. There are the usual huge state hotels in the big cities with the usual hotel luxuries. These are impersonal and expensive, especially for foreigners who have to pay more than locals, but they are where most foreigners will end up staying on any trip in Iran.

It is strictly illegal in Iran for unmarried men and women to share hotel rooms. The rule is easily enforced, as in Iran marriage is recorded in the passport. For Iranians there is no exception, although for non-Muslim foreigners the rules might be relaxed occasionally. Things are likely to be more flexible at a small pension used to backpackers than at a huge state hotel catering to Iranian families.

HEALTH
Atmospheric Pollution
The fumes in Tehran are often the major health problem for visitors as well as Tehranis. It is not a good sign to see local residents going about their business wearing hygiene masks to avoid the pollution. Respiratory problems are widespread in Tehran, especially during the winter, and asthma sufferers have a particularly difficult time. Living in such a city is not easy and anecdotal evidence suggests a good number of residents visit a psychologist (*ravashenas*) to cope with the stress levels. Outside Tehran, pollution should not be an issue and the smaller Iranian cities have excellent air as they are often high up in the mountains.

Hygiene
Standards of hygiene in Iran are generally good, indeed far better than in many neighboring countries. Certainly, Tehran is a far cleaner city than Cairo, for example. Refuse collection is well organized and the streets are refreshingly free of litter for a Middle Eastern capital. Early risers in Tehran will be impressed by the sight of hundreds of municipal workers cleaning the city before dawn.

Restaurants and snack bars are generally clean and it would appear the health authorities keep a close eye to ensure basic standards of hygiene. Meat is normally very fresh, though it is worth ensuring it has been kept in a proper fridge during summer. Sometimes, in very hot periods, the authorities will ban restaurants from selling salads in some regions for public health reasons. It is worth being careful of the Iranian yogurt drink *doogh* in summer as some shopkeepers keep their consignments in the sun outside.

Water is good to drink in almost all Iranian cities, especially in Tehran where it is said to come straight from the Alborz Mountains. However, many richer locals will only touch mineral water, which is cheaply and plentifully available in several different brands. There are a few places where the water is unsafe to drink, most notably the clerical city of Qom, where it has an uncomfortably high percentage of salt. People with sensitive stomachs would in any case feel happier drinking mineral water, given it is so cheap.

Public lavatories are not fantastic but bearable. As with all travel in this region, it is good to have liquid soap on hand for any bus journeys, during which the worst toilets are likely to be encountered. Generally, visitors can expect to leave Iran without having suffered any of the stomach problems that can bedevil visits to the Indian subcontinent.

Medical Treatment

The Iranian approach to using doctors and dentists is perhaps different from the West's. Few people in this quite fatalistic society bother with regular checkups. But if they do become sick, even with just a cold, they tend to go straight to a doctor. The idea of coping with a heavy cold simply by sitting at home and letting nature take its course is quite alien to Iranians. Doctors will often hand out prescriptions for a heavy quantity of medicines. They are also likely to offer the patient antibiotics, not only in the form of pills but as an injection. For many Iranians, it is quite normal to visit a doctor for an antibiotics injection as soon as they realize they are coming down with a cold.

Happily for this hypochondriac society, the medical profession is well trained and plentiful. If you fall sick, there should be no problem finding a doctor's office or a medical practice. Standards of dental care are also very high. There are many pharmacies (*darookhune*), which always have a huge supply of medicine. Most medicines are generics and exceedingly cheap. You will probably be given a bottle of medicine or an envelope of tablets without any instructions about use, so it is worth asking the pharmacist about the frequency of the dose and any possible side effects.

SECURITY

Iran is indisputably one of the safest countries in the Middle East for travel—at least if the question of road safety is put aside. Muggings and thefts against foreigners are extremely rare. Women find they are confronted with far less hassle than in Egypt or Turkey. Security is good. While the early days of the Islamic Republic were marred by bomb attacks and assassination attempts by the outlawed opposition, today Iran appears to enjoy stability. Bomb attacks are nowadays almost unheard-of. Generally, foreign visitors end their trip to Iran without experiencing any problems and wonder why the country has such a poor reputation abroad.

Scams

As in all big cities, petty crime can be a problem. Here there are a small number of thieves with the usual gamut of tricks. Someone could pose as a policeman and demand your passport, in a bid to steal it or extort a "fine." Never hand anything over and either walk away or demand to be taken to a police station. Police normally go out of their way not to bother foreigners and it is almost inconceivable that a bona fide officer would ask for a tourist's documents in the street. Also be aware of purse snatchers, who work at high speed from the back of motorbikes. Always make sure your backpack or camera bag is attached to both shoulders, so that it can't be pulled off. In late 2007 a French tourist was shot dead in Isfahan by a known criminal gang. The episode was striking for its rarity, and security in the once relaxed city has been ramped up in response.

Sensitive Areas

It is particularly important to exercise caution in "sensitive" areas such as military or scientific sites. The authorities do not take kindly to foreigners poking around where they are not expected. The

greatest care should also be taken
with photo or video cameras: two
Swedes recently spent over a year in
prison in Iran on accusations of
snapping military sites on the island of
Qeshm. There are major nuclear sites close to the
cities of Isfahan and Natanz but it would not be
possible to blunder into these by accident. If you
want to go somewhere very obscure (perhaps for
a special interest wildlife or bird-watching tour),
it may be wise to take a guide.

High-Risk Regions
There are also a few isolated places where it is best
not to venture, above all the southeastern Sistan-
Baluchestan province that borders Afghanistan
and Pakistan. Foreigners have been abducted in
this area in recent years by criminal gangs
involved in militant attacks and drug smuggling.
In particular, avoid the road from Bam to Quetta
in Pakistan via Zahedan, where kidnapping has
become a depressingly predictable business. All
Western embassies in Tehran issue stern warnings
about avoiding the area. In 2007 the provincial
capital Zahedan was the scene of Iran's deadliest
bomb blast in recent times when thirteen
Revolutionary Guards were killed in a bus attack
by militants. Care should also be exercised in
areas on the Iraqi and Turkish borders that have
Arab or Kurdish ethnic-minority populations,
which have been the scene of occasional separatist
militant attacks.

chapter eight

BUSINESS BRIEFING

Iran is the world's fourth-largest exporter of oil and also sits on the second-largest proven reserves of gas. It has many successful domestic firms with a long business tradition and one of the most highly educated workforces in the Middle East. So despite the political tensions of the last years, Iran has never been completely isolated from the global economy. Ties with Asian countries have always been strong while some European countries have had closer business ties with the Islamic Republic than many people would think.

THE BUSINESS ENVIRONMENT
Sanctions and the Economy
In recent years, however, economic ties between Iran and the West have become more limited. Economic links with the United States have, of course, been almost nonexistent for the last thirty years: the US administration imposed a blanket trade embargo on Iran in the aftermath of the Islamic revolution, a ban that remains in place to this day. The only exceptions are Iranian exports to the United States of the trademark Persian

goods of pistachio nuts and carpets, an exemption agreed to during a very brief and limited thaw under presidents Clinton and Khatami.

European firms have also been cutting down their business with the country in response to US pressure. Iran greatly needs foreign investment to exploit its huge oil and gas reserves but this has not been forthcoming in the necessary quantities.

Washington has also leaned on European banks to stop dealing with Iran to create another lever of pressure, meaning that at the time of writing only a handful of European banks were prepared to wire money to and from Iran. Many Iranians who are paid from abroad have been hauling in their salaries in suitcases from abroad every six months. The unilateral US measures have had a far greater economic impact than the UN Security Council sanctions imposed to punish Iran's nuclear defiance.

Foreign Firms in Iran

Despite the limitations, there are still business links between Iran and the West. First-time visitors might be surprised by the amount of Western goods available in the country, be it Tefal saucepans, Kellogg's cornflakes, or even

Coca-Cola. The cars of choice for middle-class Tehranis are likely to be Peugeots or Renaults—both mass-produced in the country in joint ventures with the national car firm Iran Khodro.

The interaction with Asia has always been greater. Iran has strong economic ties with China, South Korea, and other Asian countries including Japan, which has traditionally enjoyed good trade relations with the Islamic Republic despite its closeness to the United States. Staying in any smart Tehran hotel, it is normally quite clear that Asian businessmen far outnumber their European counterparts. Russia also has strong economic interests in Iran.

Iran's biggest trading partner is the United Arab Emirates and the booming emirate of Dubai has become a crucial hub for Iranian business. Thousands of Iranian businessmen live there and Dubai links Iran to outside markets that would otherwise be cut off by the country's relative isolation.

Foreign Currency
For years, the US dollar was by far the most widely used currency in Iranian oil transactions and for foreign currency reserves. However, the government has embarked on what appears to be a major drive to move foreign currency assets out of dollars and into euros and a lesser extent yen. This is a response to the US pressure on the Iranian financial system, which has made dollar-based transactions increasingly difficult.

Changing Money

Despite the animosity between the two governments, there is no problem exchanging US dollars. Euros are easy to change, pounds sterling a little less so outside Tehran. You are normally best advised to change money at a bureau de change—at banks, the process and the lines are likely to be long and there is no good reason to go through with this. In most cities money changing offices are widespread, although in Tehran strangely they are only to be found in the south of the city. Street changers also lurk outside and they are likely to offer a slightly better rate (though you should take extra care when handing over your dollars in the street).

THE ECONOMIC SITUATION
Inflation and Poverty

Despite the wealth of natural resources, the last years have been tough economically for Iran. Talking with ordinary people reveals that economic issues are by far their most pressing daily preoccupation. Young people may benefit from a good university education but there are often not the jobs to go around, and the result is very high youth unemployment. Prices have also surged in Iran in recent years and while the cost of basic foodstuffs may still seem very cheap compared to the West they are very *gerun* (expensive) for poorer Iranians.

Many Iranians are convinced that all Westerners are fantastically rich, and given the size of some incomes in the country they have a point. Many public-sector workers—in particular teachers, who are paid only a few hundred dollars a month—take second jobs as taxi drivers in the evenings in order to bring in sufficient money for their family. Some workers keep extremely low-paid day jobs (for example, as bus drivers) only because they offer certain social security benefits, and then try to earn some extra money in the evening in their taxis. The exhausting hours worked by many middle-aged men are a tribute to their industry and also their loyalty to their families. But foreign visitors should be tactful when discussing money matters, and to boast of a large salary or carelessly fiddle with a wad of notes could easily cause offense.

Privatization and State Control

The state retains control over around three-quarters of the economy: while there may seem to

be a large number of different companies in various sectors, they are likely to be state-owned. Ayatollah Khamenei in 2006 ordered Iran's leaders to embark on a major privatization program that would affect 80 percent of companies that were currently state-owned. The only exceptions were in the energy and defense sectors. But real signs of progress in this domain have yet to be made. The Ahmadinejad government handed out a large number of shares in privatized companies as "justice shares" to the poor, rather than to investors. Private enterprise *does* exist in Iran, and sometimes with considerable success, but so far such firms are the exception and not the rule. There has also been talk of increasing foreign participation in the economy and state-owned enterprises but again this has yet to be realized.

An increasingly important player in the economy is the elite ideological army, the Revolutionary Guards. Their economic contractors have in recent years won contracts for extensions to the Tehran metro, gas pipelines, and other major engineering projects.

DOING BUSINESS IN IRAN
Building up a Relationship

Building up a strong personal relationship is perhaps the key to doing business successfully in Iran. Iranians place great emphasis on having confidence (*etemad*) in their counterparts. This can be achieved in various ways, perhaps through activities outside the office. However, winning this trust can  take time. How easy this relationship is to establish may depend on the kind of business—the private sector is likely to prove far more easygoing and more Westernized than the state sector. Connections are extremely important, especially in the state sector, and can open doors that hitherto had seemed closed.

Arranging a Meeting

Arranging an important meeting in any business sector in Iran involves encountering the very Iranian concept of *hamahangi*. Roughly translated as "coordination," it describes the process involved in arranging and confirming any kind of meeting or interview. This may involve any number of telephone calls, faxes, and letters. This coordination process is vital to making things move ahead, especially in the state sector. When a matter is agreed to and the interview is set up, it is said to be in *hamahang* (coordinated or in harmony). However, if the necessary coordination or preparation has been lacking, it may not be possible for the meeting to take place. The importance of *hamahang* in official business in Iran is hard to exaggerate and means that long-term preparation is essential for any business visit.

In a Business Meeting

When starting any business negotiation, on no account expect to get to the point right away. The first minutes of a meeting are a time for tea drinking and pleasantries about anything other than the matter in question. Indeed, it is quite normal for nothing much to happen in a first meeting, merely a breaking of the ice; the proper business will start at the next date. Iranian counterparts will show the utmost courtesy and a foreigner's standing will grow if this is displayed in return. Forms of address are important; US-style first-name terms have not yet hit the Iranian business scene. Men should be addressed as *Agha-ye* ... (Mr. ...) and women as *Khanoom-e* ... (Ms. ...). Academic qualifications are taken seriously in Iran and it is normal to call someone with a doctorate *Agha-ye Doktor-e* ... (Mr. Doctor ...). But affection is never far away, and it is also good form to use *janam* (literally, "my dear") before the terms of formal address. So if your main interlocutor is a Dr. Jaafari you could address him as *Janam Agha-ye Doktor-e Jaafari*.

Business cards will be exchanged and this is taken seriously by Iranians. But there is no ritual ceremony of presenting them as in some Asian countries; the card needs simply to be handed over.

Dressing decently is important, but again Iran is not a country where power suits will make much difference. How you dress may depend on the people you are dealing with. Since the Islamic revolution, the uniform of choice for state employees has been a suit with an open-necked shirt or a "granddad shirt" done up to the neck. No state employee would ever wear a tie, although, as we have seen, their popularity is picking up again in the private sector.

chapter nine

COMMUNICATING

THE PERSIAN LANGUAGE

The language of Iran is Persian (Farsi) and despite the existence of several important minority languages is spoken by almost everyone in the country. For many foreigners, "Persian" conjures up the exotic and eastern. But, as we have seen, it belongs to the Indo-European family of languages—the same as most European languages like English, German, or French.

Modern Persian has its origins in the language spoken by the Indo-European Medean and Iranian tribes when they entered the area several thousand years ago. The preeminence of Persian began with Cyrus the Great and the Achaemenian dynasty. Iranians are still proud that their modern language goes back to this line of kings. It was written with the ancient wedge-shaped script of cuneiform and visitors to Iran can still admire trilingual writings in Old Persian, Babylonian, and Elamite stenciled at the ruins in the ancient capital of Persepolis. With the expansion of his realm, Darius I decreed that Aramaic should be the administrative language of the empire, but Persian was already cementing itself as the lingua franca of Iran.

The resilience of Persian in spite of centuries of linguistic invasions has been astonishing. The victory of Alexander the Great made Greek the official language of the realm under the Seleucid monarchs, a situation that was reversed when the Persian Sasanian kings came to power. But the biggest linguistic earthquake—one that still reverberates to this day—came in the seventh century with the Muslim conquest and the conversion to Islam; this ensured that Persian was written in the script of the language of the Prophet Mohammad and borrowed many of its words. To this day, Persian is written in the Arabic alphabet, with a few additional letters. Even more linguistic turbulence came with

the raids of the Turkic-speaking Mongols. The 1979 Islamic revolution further accentuated the use of Arabic words and structures in Persian.

But despite these invasions, Persian has retained its distinct Indo-European identity to this day. First-time learners are normally struck by the similarities with European languages. Mother is *mader*, father is *pedar*, girl is *dokhtar*, water is *ab* (related to Latin "aqua"), and bad is simply *bad*. Grammatical structures are hardly alien, for example conjugating the verb "to go" in the present tense brings familiar verb endings (*miravam, miravi, miravad, miravim, miravid, miravand*).

However, the situation is not all straightforward. As we have seen, Persian is written in a lightly adapted version of the Arabic alphabet and is read from right to left. The alphabet is tricky, given that the characters change their shape depending on whether they are at the beginning, middle, or end of a word; the vowels are often not indicated, leaving just the consonants. While Persian's Indo-European origins are still evident, Arabic has left its mark with its distinctive structures and large vocabulary. These can be difficult for Westerners to learn. Many Persian teachers believe it is hard to become fluent in modern Persian without some knowledge of Arabic.

COMMUNICATING IN EVERYDAY LIFE
Finding English Speakers

Very basic communication in Iran is not too difficult but expressing more complex ideas may require considerable language training. Most people in Iran do not speak English, although in a country with such high educational standards you will find many city dwellers who do. Don't be surprised if an assertive woman—even one who is conservatively dressed—comes bounding up to you to show off her fluent English or French. Given the lack of opportunities available to practice their language skills, English speakers will often find visitors rather than the other way around. Generally the further away you are from a major city, the less chance you have of finding an English speaker. But in Iran, more than anywhere else, the unexpected is always possible.

Helpfully, all signs on major highways are written in Persian and English. Road signs in Tehran are also normally bilingual, frequent, and reliable. Outside the most touristy areas, you are very unlikely to find a menu in English, so you will have to ask the waiter what is available.

Speaking Persian

Mastering some basic words and phrases (see Chapter 4) will ensure instant popularity. Iranians are immensely proud of their language and how it has retained its difference from Arabic, which is even less widely spoken than English outside the clerical elite. The language also boasts a great literature, most famously in the work of the sensual medieval poets Hafez and Saadi but also in modern novels and poetry. Poetry is still important in daily life; it is not unusual to be stuck in a Tehran traffic jam and find the taxi driver suddenly reciting the verses of Hafez. Imagine being in London traffic and the driver suddenly waxing lyrical over a Shakespeare sonnet!

Persian Outside Iran

Iran is not the only country where Persian is spoken—it is the lingua franca of neighboring Afghanistan, where the dialect is known as Dari and is spoken by educated people of whatever ethnicity. Dari is intelligible to Persian speakers but strong accents and different words can make this difficult for outsiders. Persian is also the official language of the former Soviet republic of Tajikistan, where it is known as Tajik and is written in the Russian Cyrillic script. In both cases, the language is likely to have been spread by Persian-speaking soldiers forming the backbone of the armies that brought Islam to these countries in the later Arab invasions. Persian was also chosen as the court language of India under the Turkic Mughals, a situation that lasted right until British colonization.

GESTURES

Gestures are important to Iranians and many people wave their hands animatedly when in a conversation or an argument. But in this ultra-polite society there are a number of set gestures, most notably ones that imply respect toward a conversation partner. If an Iranian touches both palms to the forehead, this is a sign of great respect toward the person with whom they are talking. One gesture to avoid is the Western thumbs-up sign: in Iran, it is an obscene gesture and loosely translates as "up yours."

HUMOR

Iranians revel in humor, be it the slapstick comedies broadcast on television or something more sophisticated. The growth of the Internet and mobile communications has also had an effect on humor and extremely subtle jokes, frequently about politics, transmitted by SMS have become enormously popular throughout the country. Iranians also enjoy making jokes about the various ethnic groups that make up the country, such as the Turkic population in the north. Even individual towns have acquired particular connotations—the city of Qazvin is said to be full of homosexuals while the women of the northern town of Rasht have a reputation for being wayward.

THE MEDIA
State Television

Television broadcasting in Iran has been monopolized by state channels. The programing is consequently often uninspiring, although the state broadcaster has been taking steps to rectify this in recent years. There are seven TV channels that can usually be picked up in Iranian cities, including one for sports and young people, a twenty-four-hour news network, a local channel, and a Koran channel. The main channels show plenty of news and also footage of the Islamic revolution, the war against Iraq, and religious services to inspire the faithful. Sports are well covered and soccer fans will be delighted to know that English Premiership and La Liga games as well as European matches are broadcast live.

Soap operas are wildly popular, especially over the fasting month of Ramazan, and are likely to form one of the main topics of conversation in Tehran cafés. They tend to last for a dozen episodes and feature actors and actresses who are genuine stars in the country. A real effort has been made to give such dramas greater audience appeal and issues relating to love now feature prominently. Previously taboo subjects are now being tackled, be it the temptation of love affairs or, in the case of the groundbreaking 2007 hit *Zero Degree Turn*, the Holocaust. The state broadcaster has also been trying to keep audiences happy by showing an increasing number of foreign films, which sometimes appear just months after they come out in cinemas in the West. English-language programing is limited, although there are TV news broadcasts in English twice a day.

Satellite Television

No private channels exist in Iran. This does not prevent a number of normally US-based channels seeking to beam their signals into the country, much to the displeasure of the authorities who regard such broadcasts as anti-regime propaganda. The most prominent such channel is the Persian service of the Voice of America, while Radio Free Europe/Liberty also has a Persian-language radio station known as Radio Farda. The BBC is also to launch a Persian-language television channel, an idea that has received a lukewarm reception from Iranian officials. There are also many music channels pumping out the no-holds-barred Persian pop produced in Los Angeles and elsewhere.

In order to combat what they see as hostile broadcasting, the authorities have made satellite dishes illegal in Iran. They say the foreign-based Persian stations, as well as the other channels that can be picked up by satellite, risk polluting the public mind. The measure remains in force and the police periodically patrol neighborhoods and confiscate the illicit dishes lurking on the roofs of housing blocks. However, many people still flout the law in Tehran and if their dish is confiscated merely put up another one. Strangely, it is possible to watch BBC World and CNN in most top-end hotels, including state-run ones. But there is little chance of the official situation changing in the near future.

State broadcasting (IRIB) also runs its own array of satellite channels for foreigners. Two channels show Iranian television programs to the outside world, often with subtitles. There is the slick and successful Al-Alam, an Arabic-language news channel that is popular with Shiites outside Iran. IRIB's latest innovation, launched in 2007, is Press-TV, an English-language satellite channel that broadcasts round-the-clock news combined with current affairs news documentaries. Its avowed aim is to break the Western stranglehold on the world's media by giving an Iran-based version of world events.

Radio

The state radio channels offer a choice of
traditional music, talk, sports, or religion. The
most popular choices in Tehran at present appear
to be Radio Javan (88.1 FM), which has
surprisingly open discussions of many issues
(listen in also for its hyperactive female
presenters), and Radio Payam (107.7), which has
music punctuated by news bulletins and all-
important traffic information every fifteen
minutes.

The Press

Despite state pressure and dozens of closures, the
press in Iran remains one of the liveliest in the
Middle East. The reformist liberal press had its
heyday in the early years of the Khatami
presidency, but hard-liners subsequently closed
down dozens of papers and even arrested
journalists. There have been further closures in
recent years and pressure from the state
continues, but this has not stopped papers
relaunching under a different name or new

publications emerging. The liberal
Iranian papers contain impressively
learned articles about the latest
films, international affairs, or
scientific trends. They are also not
afraid to criticize the government,
especially on the economy, and the
comments can on occasion be quite cutting. But
they have to obey certain rules. In 2007 the

leading moderate daily *Shargh* (East) was shut down after it published an interview with a well-known expatriate Iranian lesbian.

Reformist Newspapers

At the time of writing, the best moderate papers are *Etemad* (Confidence), *Etemad Melli* (National Confidence), *Kargozaran* (Executives), and *Sarmayeh* (Treasury). They all have an attractive layout and biting articles about politics and society. The weekly *Shahrvand* (Citizen) is a glossy publication that has become required reading for the Iranian intelligentsia. However, all this information can change very fast, as closures followed by new apparitions are always possible. The most widely read papers are often the numerous sports dailies that feed the appetite for news about the national obsession with soccer.

Hard-line Newspapers

At the other end of the spectrum are the hard-line papers that stress their loyalty to the revolution and hostility to Western governments in every column inch. The best-known is the fiercely ideological *Kayhan* (Universe), whose editor is appointed by the supreme leader and whose editorials are required reading to understand what hard-liners are thinking. The slightly more moderate *Jomhouri Eslami* (Islamic Republic) follows a similar line. The hardest hard-line daily of them all is the somewhat batty *Siasat-e Rouz* (Politics of the Day), which has a particular dislike of Britain and especially its ownership of verdant embassy compounds in Tehran.

English-language Newspapers
There are four English-language dailies—*Tehran Times, Iran Daily, Iran News,* and *Kayhan International*—but they are nowhere near as informative as the Persian-language newspapers. However, they do have the virtue of being easily obtainable at most Tehran newsstands. Buying Western newspapers or magazines is hard in Iran. Even if they are available (perhaps in a hotel shop), they are likely to be out-of-date, overpriced, and perhaps even lightly censored.

INTERNET AND TELECOMMUNICATIONS
Internet
Internet access is not at all bad in Iran; several service providers offer broadband and there are a number of Internet cafés. There is one major caveat: the state telecommunications authorities block hundreds of Web sites deemed to be hostile to the country or bad for public morality. These include obvious ones like the Web sites of outlawed opposition groups or previously banned newspapers, as well as some more mainstream Web sites. There are also sites that appear to be blocked despite apparently being innocuous.

Telephones

It is easy to dial direct from a hotel or private home abroad but you cannot do this from a public phone box. The mobile phone network has improved greatly over recent years thanks to the emergence of a second operator competing with the state monopoly (previously making a single call could take several attempts), but telephoning may still require a little persistence.

MAIL

Postal services are reliable but sending letters and packages to the West can be a little slow. However, international courier services like DHL do have a presence in Tehran. For sending letters inside the city, many Iranians use a motorbike courier (*peyk*), which is quick and relatively inexpensive.

CONCLUSION

Visiting Iran is a full-scale assault on the senses and the intellect. The country's rich history— both pre- and post-Islam—is apparent both in people's behavior and the architectural heritage. The streets beat with the dynamism of a fast-changing society that has witnessed huge political, social, and demographic upheavals over the last half century. Iranian women are among the most opinionated and ambitious in the Middle East. Preconceptions about the country are exploded on every street corner. Social behavior is often very different from the West—but also surprisingly similar. The official hostile rhetoric toward the West contrasts with the extraordinary openness and hospitality of the people.

This book has attempted to be a guide to the contradictions, complexities, and delights of this extraordinary country that has been misunderstood by outsiders for far too long. Some Iranians say that they have given up trying to understand their own country—but that does not mean that outsiders should not try. Surprises and stimulation await anyone willing to visit Iran for the first time.

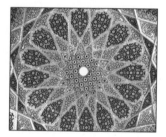

Further Reading

de Bellaigue, Christopher. *In the Rose Garden of Martyrs: A Memoir of Iran*. London: Harper Perennial, 2005.

Byron, Robert. *The Road to Oxiana*. London: Penguin, 2007.

Curtis, John. *Ancient Persia*. London: British Museum Press, 2000.

Digard, Jean-Pierre, and Bernard Hourcade and Yann Richard. *L'Iran au XXe siècle*. Paris: Fayard, 2007.

Ebadi, Shirin. *Iran Awakening*. London: Rider, 2007.

Farzad, Narguess. *Modern Persian*. London: Hodder Headline, 2004.

Firouz, Eskander. *The Complete Fauna of Iran*. London: I. B. Tauris, 2005.

Gheissari, Ali, and Vali Nasr, *Democracy in Iran. History and the Quest for Liberty*. Oxford: Oxford University Press, 2006.

Issa, Rose, and Sheila Whitaker (eds). *Life and Art. The New Iranian Cinema*. National Film Theatre/British Film Institute: London, 1999.

Keddie, Nikki R. *Modern Iran*. New Haven, Conn.: Yale, 2006.

Kinzer, Stephen. *All The Shah's Men*. Hoboken, N.J.: Wiley, 2003.

Mottahedeh, Roy. *The Mantle of the Prophet*. Oxford: One World, 2000.

Naipul, V. S. *Beyond Belief*. London: Little Brown, 1998.

Nasr, Vali. *The Shia Revival: How Conflicts Within Islam Will Shape the Future*. London: W. W. Norton, 2006.

Sadr, Hamid Reza. *Iranian Cinema, A Political History*. London: I. B. Tauris, 2006.

Shaida, Margaret. *The Legendary Cuisine of Persia*. London: Grub Street, 2000.

Thackston, Wheeler M. *An Introduction to Persian*. Bethsheda, Md.: Ibex, 1993.

culture smart! iran

Index

Acknowledgment

This book is for my mum and dad, with love and gratitude.